MW01226804

spiritual realities

Volume 2

THE BREATH
OF
GOD
IN US

by
Harold R. Eberle

Spiritual Realities Volume II:
The Breath of God in Us

Copyright © 1997

Winepress Publishing
P.O. Box 10653
Yakima, WA 98909-1653
1-800-308-5837

Library of Congress Catalog Card No. 97-060374
ISBN 1-882523-08-3

Cover by Jeff Boettcher
Graphic Art by Diane Buchanan and Eugene M. Holmes

All Biblical quotations are taken from the *New American Standard Bible*
© 1977, The Lockman Foundation, La Habra, California 90631. (Unless
otherwise noted).

ALL RIGHTS RESERVED

No part of this publication may be reproduced, stored in a retrieval
system, or transmitted in any form or by any means — electronic,
mechanical, photocopy, recording, or otherwise — without the express
prior permission of Winepress Publishing Company, with the exception of
brief excerpts in magazine articles and/or reviews.

Requests for translating into other languages should be addressed to
Winepress Publishing.

Printed in the United States of America

Dedication and Thanks

This book would not have been possible if it had not been for Pastor Jim Leuschian of Spokane, Washington, who helped me think through the many doctrinal issues and challenged me on numerous points. His theological insight brought me back down to earth and forced me to communicate spiritual principles in understandable terms.

Also, I had input and editing advice from R. E. McMaster, Ken Kolman, Martha Brookhart, Peter Eisenmann, John Frady, and Dennis Jacobson. Annette Bradley deserves special mention for her expertise in the area of editing and preparing the final copy. Each of these have left their mark on these pages and on my life.

However, I owe most to my staff who have faithfully given their time month by month and served in love over the last five years: Linda (my wife), Mike and Maria Clark, Mike and Maribel Pillsbury, Shane and Barbara Donaldson, Dave and Diane Buchanan, Tad and Michele Romberger, and Ken and Robbie Kolman. I ask the people who read these words to pray for my staff, their marriages, children, lives and walks with God.

Table of Contents

Introduction

The contents of these volumes build upon one another progressively. We continually will be expanding our concept of the spiritual world and our relationship to it. Because of new truths, perspectives, and terms constantly being introduced, it is vital that you work through these writings in the sequence they are presented. It is too easy to misunderstand subjects as serious and critical as these. Therefore, we ask that you become familiar with the foundations that were laid in Volume I, before delving into this volume.

In Volume I, we established a basic understanding of the spiritual world. We discussed the laws which govern that realm and how they are different from the laws governing the natural realm. We explained the existence of two kingdoms in the spiritual realm: God's and Satan's. And then we explained how people may gain access to the spiritual world, enabling them to release power, blessings, or curses into this natural world. Finally, we gave a basis for discerning what is of God and what is not: (1) fruit manifesting over the long term; (2) agreement with the written Word of God; and (3) the exaltation of Jesus Christ as Lord.

In this volume, we turn our attention to the nature of man and his relationship with the spiritual world. Only as we have an accurate understanding of man's spirit, soul, and body, can we give clear explanations for the spiritual and supernatural phenomena seen in the world around us.

The Origin of Man's Spirit and Soul

In the beginning, God's Spirit was brooding over the surface of the earth, preparing it for His creative acts to follow. After He spoke into existence the various elements of our world, He went to work on His greatest creation: man.

In the Book of Genesis, we read how God created the first man, Adam:

> And the Lord God formed man
> of the dust of the ground, and
> breathed into his nostrils the
> breath of life; and man became
> a living soul (Gen. 2:7- KJV).

Identify three different elements involved in Adam's being: the body formed from dust, the breath released from God, and the soul which was created.

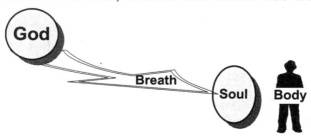

The Breath of God in Us

The body is, of course, the physical element with which we are most familiar. The soul is the created element — it came into existence at a point in time. And the word *breath often* is interpreted with the word *spirit.* It is that breath of God which we see going into man and forming his spirit.

In the New Testament we can read about the same three elements in man's being. For example, the Apostle Paul wrote:

> Now may the God of peace Himself sanctify you entirely; and may your spirit and soul and body be preserved complete, without blame at the coming of our Lord Jesus Christ (I Thess. 5:23).

Notice how this verse mentions all three parts of man's being.

Some Christian teachers today believe that the soul and the spirit within a person are the same thing. They envision the soul as being fashioned out of the spiritual breath of God, much like the dust of the earth was used to form the physical body. If that is true, then the terms spirit and soul refer to the same substance within man and should be thought of as one and the same. Christian teachers who think this way recognize only two parts to man's being: the physical body and a spirit/soul. This two-part view of man is called *dichotomous,* a word simply meaning *two parts.*

In contrast, the word *trichotomous* is used to talk about the view which portrays man as a three-part being. The trichotomous teacher emphasizes that the spirit and the soul remain as separate entities within a person.

No one really knows for sure in what way the spirit was used to bring the soul of man into existence. Creative acts are beyond our full comprehension. What we have to help us understand the nature of man are numerous Bible passages which talk about the various activities and functions of man's being.

There are some verses in the Bible which refer to persons having three distinct parts (i.e., I Thess. 5:23). Other verses indicate that man has only two parts, a natural part and a spiritual part (i.e., I Cor. 7:34; Matt. 26:41). Therefore, we must see man as being both dichotomous and trichotomous. In one sense, he is a two-part being, because the spirit and the soul are so intertwined that in many ways they are one. We may be able to separate them for discussion purposes, but in reality the spiritual substance of God's breath in some fashion was used to actually bring the soul of man into existence.

At the same time, when speaking in other contexts, we can talk about the spirit of man as being separate from the soul. For example, we separate the two when talking about their origin — the spirit coming from God's breath and the soul being created. Because the spirit came from God, we will see later how this "God stuff" within us has certain characteristics not associated with the created soul.

We also must separate them when talking from God's perspective, because several verses mention how God could withdraw His breath from men if He chose to do so. For example Job 34:14-15 tells us:

> "If He [God] should determine
> to do so,
> If He should gather to Himself
> His Spirit and His breath,
> All flesh would perish together,
> And man would turn to dust."

Because God could withdraw the spirit from man, we must recognize the spirit as separate from the soul when looking from His viewpoint.

We do not want to make this seem complicated. We simply are pointing out that both dichotomous and trichotomous views fail if we limit ourselves to just one or the other. The Bible has Scriptures speaking from both perspectives. That is the reason why some Christian teachers today teach one way and some take the other perspective.

In the following pages, when we talk about the spirit as an entity separate from the soul, we are speaking of that spiritual energy which both originated from the breath of God and is resident within man. When we speak of the soul/spirit we are talking about the two elements which function together as one. And then as we talk about the soul only, we are doing this for the purpose of understanding; but please keep in mind that the soul does not exist independently of the spirit which sustains it.

In the next chapter, we will begin examining the nature and functions of the soul and spirit within man. But first we need to establish the origin of man's spirit.

It is not just Adam in whom God's breath resides. Every human being has this spiritual breath from God. In the passage from the Book of Job which we last quoted (34:14-15), we read that all flesh would perish if God were to withdraw His Spirit from man. If God simply *inhaled* His breath from mankind, we would all turn to dust. From Scriptures such as these we learn of the *life-sustaining function* of the spirit within man (see also Eccl. 12:7 and Job 33:4), and we also conclude that God's breath is in every human being.

We can understand that God breathed life into the first man, but how does it actually get into all other human beings?

Think of the breath which God released into Adam. We understand that in that initial breath God *fathered* not just Adam, but all of mankind. The Lord is referred to in the Bible as the "God of the spirits of all flesh" (Num. 16:22;27:16) and the "Father of spirits" (Heb. 12:9). God is the Originator, the Source, the starting point for all of life. The spiritual substance which God released into Adam became the substance of life which energized all of mankind.

Consider the power in that first breath. Compare it with God's other creative acts, such as when He spoke into existence the plant life in this world. In God's spoken words, "Let the earth bring forth vegetation," there was enough power to give life to all plants for the duration of this world. In a corresponding way, there was enough power in the divine breath that was released into Adam to give life to all the generations that would follow him.

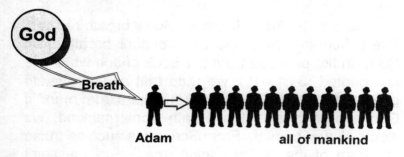

The *residue of God's breath* abides in every living human being. By using the word *residue,* we do not want to imply that the amount within the later generations is diminished. Rather, the spiritual substance of life is creative and, hence, reproduced in every single human being.

It is important for us to recognize that God began the entire human race through Adam. The Apostle Paul explained in the New Testament:

> "The God who made the world
> and all things in it, since He is
> Lord of heaven and earth....He

Himself gives to all life and breath and all things; and <u>He made from one</u>, every nation of mankind to live on all the face of the earth, having determined their appointed times, and the boundaries of their habitation.... Being then the offspring of God..." (Acts 17:24-29 — emphasis added).

Notice that every human being is considered the *offspring of God,* having been made from the one man, Adam.

It is critical that we establish in our minds the truth that the spiritual substance of life originated with the breath of God, and that it is passed on through generational lines. Even today, the spirit which sustains life in a newborn baby originated with that first breath released into Adam.

It is at this point that some people have a misconception. They wrongly imagine God releasing spiritual life into the womb of a mother each time there is conception, or at some point during the gestation period. That is a common misunderstanding, and we need to establish the fact here that the *spirit-substance* of life itself is passed through the generational lines.

The passing on of spiritual substance from one generation to another is made clear when we study the account concerning Abraham and Levi in Hebrews 7:9-10. We are told that when Abraham brought his offering to God, Levi was "in the loins" of

Abraham. Levi did not come down to the earth from heaven and then enter the womb of his mother. No. Notice the *location* of Levi. The Bible tells us that he was *in the loins* of his great-great-grandfather. The amazing thing is that Levi was not born until four generations later.

We are not saying that Levi fully existed before his conception, but the spiritual substance, indeed, did exist within his forefather. Levi's soul, the created element, would not have come into existence until the spiritual substance came in contact with the physical substance in the womb of his mother.

We can make a comparison at this point. Since the spirit is seen as the energy which sustains life, think of an electric current flowing through wires to a light bulb. The wires are compared with the generational lines, and the light bulb is at the point where a person comes into existence.

The question, "When does human life begin?" has some profound implications when we consider many of the issues facing today's society. Having a Biblical understanding determines much of what we believe about abortion, genetic engineering, etc.

Concerning this, notice what King David said as he praised God,

For Thou didst form my inward
parts;
Thou didst weave me in my
mother's womb....
Thine eyes have seen my
unformed substance;
And in Thy book they were all
written,
The days that were ordained
for me,
When as yet there was not one
of them
(Ps. 139:13-16).

Notice that God has ordained a set time for each person's existence. God established these times before this world was made. The spiritual substance of life pre-existed with God from the beginning, and we were each in the thoughts of God. However, the soul of man comes into existence simultaneously as the body is formed within the womb of the mother. That time is set by God.

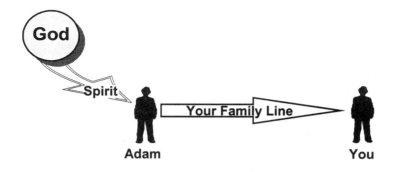

The Breath of God in Us

We can summarize this first chapter by saying that all human beings depend upon the breath of God to sustain their life. That breath originated from the first breath released into Adam. Through Adam, God fathered all of mankind.

The only exception to this was the birth of Jesus. He was *born of the Holy Spirit* as the Spirit came upon the virgin Mary (Luke 1:26-35). He descended directly from heaven as the Word became flesh (John 1:14; 6:46-51; 8:23, 42). Jesus was the "only begotten Son" of God (John 3:16). In contrast, all the rest of mankind have been naturally born of Adam.

The Nature of Man's Spirit and Soul

What do the soul and spirit look like? As we answer this, keep in mind that every human being — Christians and non-Christians — has a soul and a spirit. Later, we will explain how the spirit of a Christian is different from the spirit of a non-Christian. Here we will consider the basic structure of the soul and spirit.

The soul (in contrast to the spirit) has a definite shape and size. We understand that it is structured like the human body. There are several reasons we believe this.

First, the Bible associates the soul with the blood which is flowing throughout man's body (i.e., Gen. 9:4; Lev. 17:11-14; Deut. 12:23). As the blood saturates every part of man's physical body, we understand that the soul does, too. The soul is not existing in the blood physically, but it is an invisible, spiritual entity corresponding to the blood. Therefore it is best to think of the soul as filling the body.

The Breath of God in Us

We also can see the structure and shape of the soul as we study Bible passages which describe the human soul, particularly after it has left the body due to death. For example, in First Samuel 28:8-19, we read the story of how King Saul had a medium conjure up the prophet Samuel from the dead. This is obviously an evil exercise forbidden by God, but we can note from this Bible account, how the Prophet Samuel appeared in the form of an old man (vs. 13-14). We also can see this "soul shape" in Luke 16:19-31, where our Lord told a story of Lazarus and a rich man in Hades. In this passage, He referred to the *finger of Lazarus* and the *tongue of the rich man,* even though both were separated from their physical bodies. The two in Hades even were able to recognize each other. Therefore, facial features of the natural man must be evident upon the soul. We can conclude from such accounts that if we were able to see the soul with our natural eyes, it would appear as the body, having arms, legs, facial features, and every other part.

Soul   **Body**

Although at times we will diagram the soul as being separate from the body, as above, keep in mind that the soul is actually superimposed over and filling the same location as the physical body.

Contrast this now with the spirit of man. If we were to talk about the spirit independently of the soul, we would not describe it as having shape or size (as we understand shape and size in the natural sense). Of course, the spirit fills and gives life to the soul and body, but it comes from the breath of God. As such, it is the *God stuff* in each of us. Because it is divine in origin, it is wrong to define man's spirit in natural terms of shape or size. Throughout these writings, we at times may draw the human spirit in some shape, but do not limit your thoughts or conclusions to the point of believing that one may put this divinely originated energy into a natural container.

Spirit   **Soul**   **Body**

In talking about the spirit of man, the Bible makes several comparisons with light and energy. We will examine some of these comparisons as we continue using terms such as "life-energy" or "substance of life." These terms may sound somewhat mystical, or perhaps too much like terms being used by various cults today. We do not want to borrow any of their vocabulary, nor present any non-Biblical concepts. However, it is the Bible which teaches us how the spirit of man sustains life. It compares the spirit with both energy and light. Therefore, we will use these references as we continue.

Still, we must not limit our understanding of the spirit to concepts related to energy or light, nor to any other natural comparison that we can make. Comparisons are never the real thing. They can help us understand some of the functions of the spirit, but they never can give us the whole picture. Energy, for example, is something which functions in this natural world according to natural laws. The spirit is of the spiritual world. Since it is the *God stuff* resident in each of us, it does not function according to the natural laws which govern this world. As we continue, we will learn that the spirit of man is not limited in space and that it, indeed, can reach beyond the physical body of a person (Volumes IV to VII). Therefore, in order to understand this spiritual substance resident in man, we must not limit ourselves to natural comparisons.

It is helpful at this point to establish the *flowing* nature of the spirit within man. The spirit is not a stagnant structure. It is more accurate to think of it as *moving energy*, flowing from within a person's innermost being. The Book of Proverbs talks about this energy, explaining that from the heart "flow the springs of life" (Prov. 4:23). Jesus likened this to rivers flowing within a person and issuing forth all of life.

Spirit   Soul   Body

Finally, let's examine the difference between the spirit of the Christian and the spirit of the non-Christian. Jesus explained that he who believes in Him would have rivers of *living* water flowing from his innermost being (John 7:38). Both Christians and non-Christians have a spirit which sustains their life and flows within them, but the rivers within the believer consist of *living* water. In another Bible passage, our Lord explained that those who came to Him would have a "well of water springing up to eternal life" (John 4:14). It is this *life* which we must identify as a quality unique to the spirit of the Christian.

When God created Adam, He gave Adam the opportunity to sin. God first warned Adam that in the day he sinned, he would die (Gen. 2:17). When Adam sinned in the Garden of Eden, he did not die physically, but we understand that a certain spiritual death came over him. In the New Testament we are told that Adam's sin released death into the world and that death spread to all of mankind (Rom. 5:12).

When a person commits his life to the Lordship of Jesus, the presence of Jesus enters his spirit. His spirit is then made *alive unto God.* The Apostle Paul explained:

> And if Christ is in you...the spirit
> is alive because of righteous-
> ness (Rom. 8:10).

God intervenes in the life of a person when he receives Jesus. At that time new life is breathed into his spirit.

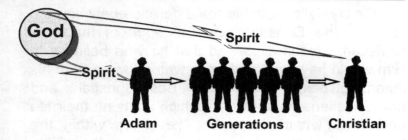

God | Spirit | Spirit

Adam | Generations | Christian

We identify this introduction of new spiritual life as the experience of being "born again." We each have been born naturally as descendants of Adam. We inherit from him spiritual energy, but because of sin, there is a sentence of death carried with that spiritual substance. When we submit our lives to Jesus Christ, we are born into the family of God. The rivers within us then become as living waters.

In summary, we can say that both Christians and non-Christians have a soul and spirit. The soul is structured like the human body. The spirit is the flowing, moving energy which sustains life. The spirit within the believer has a quality of life related to its association with God — it is alive to God!

Identifying
Emotions and Thoughts

As we develop our understanding of man, always keep in mind that man is a whole person. We have introduced the terms *dichotomist* and *trichotomist* in reference to the differing views of man's nature. Unfortunately, if we embrace either one of these labels, we tend to form images in our minds of a person being divided into the corresponding parts. Those images are misleading because man is a united being. I would prefer to be considered a *monochotomist*, emphasizing one part. With that label we focus on man's existence as a single person who functions as a unit.

Spirit/Soul/Body

It is a fact that we should not divide man into two or three parts, thinking that any one of those parts functions independently of the other parts. Whatever happens to the spirit influences the soul and the body. What happens to the soul affects the spirit and the body. And even what influences the body influences the spirit and the soul. It is best to keep in mind that man is a unit, all parts being interdependent upon one another.

Some Christians miss this truth. They wrongly try to compartmentalize the various functions of man's being. Concluding that man is a three-part being, they try to assign various functions just to the body, just to the soul, or just to the spirit. Such thinking is wrong.

Let's identify certain elements within man and see how they exist throughout his being. Here we will locate his emotions and thoughts.

First, consider man's emotions. Some have tried to assign human emotions only to the soul of man. That is false.

We know that the physical body shows emotional responses with various physiological changes and biochemical reactions. Scientists actually can measure these changes in bodily functions as emotions are aroused.

In the Bible we also can see verses which attribute emotions to both the soul and the spirit. For instance, Psalm 42:11 tells us of emotional turmoil within the soul, while First Kings 21:5 speaks of sadness of spirit. Luke 1:47 tells us of joy coming from the human spirit, while Psalms 94:19 and 103:1-2 speak of joy within the soul of man. In John 13:21 we are told that our Lord Jesus was troubled in spirit, while Matthew 26:38 tells us He was deeply grieved in His soul. From these and many other verses in both the Old and New Testaments, we have to conclude that emotions cannot be assigned to only one part of man's being, but they are rooted throughout.

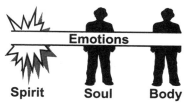

This feature of man's emotional existence is even more interesting when we consider certain physical stimuli on the human body. For example, when depressant drugs are injected into the bloodstream of an individual, his entire being is affected. Not just his physical body lowers in its energy level, but his spirit and soul are also influenced. Similarly, there are hallucinogenic drugs that may open a person's entire being to the spiritual dimension. There are other drugs which can cause the sexual passions to be aroused. Electrical impulses on certain parts of the nervous system can trigger similar responses. It is a fact that any feeling or emotion can be stirred throughout a person's being by the use of certain chemical or electrical stimulations.

Emotions also can be stirred *from the other side*. By this we mean that spiritual influences acting upon a person's spirit may cause responses in his soul and physical body. For example, as God's Spirit comes upon a person, he may feel it physically. A devil may come to an individual causing physiological changes to occur, as well as causing an emotional reaction of fear, hate, bitterness, etc. Emotions, then, are not just physical in origin but also spiritual.

To make this picture complete, we also must say that emotions may arise through activities within the soul of man. A man who is in financial trouble, because he has lost his job, may begin meditating upon his situation to the extent that his spirit and bodily functions are altered. Thoughts and desires centered within the soul may influence a person in every area of his being.

Our main point here is that emotions exist throughout a person's entire being, and whatever happens in one part influences all.

In the same way, we can identify certain thought processes occurring on all three levels.

To see this, first consider the human body. Your brain processes information, makes simple decisions and sends millions of electrical impulses coursing through your nervous system throughout each day. Your brain is deciding how warm to keep your body, how much food to digest, where to send more blood, etc. Millions of thoughts are being processed every minute. The related biochemical reactions all are associated with various thought processes occurring on the level of your physical being.

These physical processes correlate with what is going on in the soul/spirit: the soul/spirit influencing what thought processes happen in the brain, and the brain influencing what is happening in the spirit/soul.

When we talk about thought processes within the soul, we usually are referring to the more conscious decisions we make. As we explained in Volume I, the word *mind* usually is used when speaking of the location of our thought processes within our soul. The brain is the organ through which our mind has contact with the natural world.

Soul   Body

When we talk about the spirit, we see the function of inspiration, visions, creativity, etc. We have explained that the spirit is the life-energy within a person, and as such it enables a person to think. The Apostle Paul posed the question:

> For who among men knows the thoughts of a man except the spirit of the man, which is in him? (I Cor. 2:11a).

The obvious answer to this question is, "No one." It is the spirit within a person which illuminates his being and reveals his thoughts. It is helpful to view the spirit in this sense, as a light shining within a person, illuminating his own thoughts.

Soul   Body

The Breath of God in Us

There is a fundamental difference here between the life of the Christian and the non-Christian. The spirit within the believer has been made alive unto God. Therefore, the energy flowing from within his innermost being will cause his thoughts to come more and more into alignment with God's thoughts. Paul explained that the natural man cannot understand the things of God, because his spirit has not been changed within (I Cor. 2:10-14). However, the Christian has the ongoing work of the Holy Spirit within his spirit to reveal the thoughts of God (I Cor. 2:9-10). In the Book of Proverbs we read that "The spirit of a man is the lamp of the Lord" (Prov. 20:27a). It is through the spirit that God shines His light, revealing His thoughts.

From this point forward it will be helpful if you keep in mind the function of the spirit in enabling a person to think. It shines from within as a light. Or we can think of it as a river rising from within, bathing the thought processes and giving inspiration. The spirit is the energy quickening the mind.

Our main point here is that the entire man — spirit, soul and body — is involved in thinking processes.

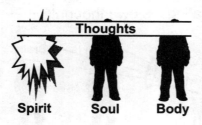

Spirit   **Soul**   **Body**

For final evidence of this, consider the person with a severe headache brought on by worry. Worry does not happen independently within the soul or spirit. The body is involved, and variations in electrical impulses within the brain actually can be measured with electronic instruments. Likewise, the headache can hinder deeper thought processes, and a person may be unable to make wise decisions. Certain pain-relieving drugs may be ingested into the body, causing the headache to disappear. Then the spirit/soul is freed to function as intended. Or the headache may at times be decreased as a person relaxes and changes the focus of his inner thoughts. What we see is that the body influences the spirit/soul and the spirit/soul influences the body.

We will talk more in coming pages about man's existence as a unit. In the next chapter, we even will show that man's will and heart exist on all three levels: spirit, soul, and body. Picture at this point man as a whole person, functioning as a unit throughout his entire being. This is the Biblical view of how God created man.

Spirit/Soul/Body

The Breath of God in Us

4

Identifying the
Will and Heart

It is time to locate and identify the will and heart of man. In Chapter 3 we explained how man must be seen as a whole person, with various functions permeating his entire being. We stated that it is wrong to try to compartmentalize man's various functions or limit them to just the body, just the soul, or just the spirit. In particular, we saw this in relationship to the emotions and thought processes of man. Here we will see that this truth also applies to the will and heart of man.

As we explain this, I must ask you to approach it with a fresh perspective. Many of my readers have already spent time researching these issues and they have studied the writings of various other leaders. Different teachers have had slightly differing views on the nature of man and the various functions of his being. If you already have fixed in your mind specific teachings, it will be very difficult for you to fit in truths that are new to you. The more convinced a person already has become, the harder it is for him to see from another perspective. Therefore, what I am asking you to do is to let go of your present under-standings on these issues for just a few minutes. If you already have an established way of looking at the nature of man, please set it aside temporarily, so at least your mind will be open to consider whether the following makes sense, and, indeed, agrees with the Bible. Then, if you disagree, you can go back to your way of thinking after we are done. But at least for a few minutes, I ask of you the privilege to communicate with you fairly. Please give me that chance here.

First, consider man's will. Where is it located?

Some people have taught that the will is within the soul of man. Others try to locate it in the spirit. And those who see man as merely a physical being usually conclude that man's will is within his brain. Who is right? They all are to some degree. The will of man permeates his entire being.

To see this, first identify the decisions made at the level of the body. There are hundreds of biochemical processes going on inside of you right now, all governed by the dictates of your brain.

You can influence some of the natural processes from a deeper level within your being. For example, you can make a conscious decision at the level of your spirit/soul not to sleep. However, the demands of the physical body eventually will overrule your conscious mind.

Consider the control of your breathing. You are capable of making a conscious decision right now to stop breathing. In that case, your inner man is to some degree ruling over the natural governing processes of your body. However, you cannot hold your breath indefinitely. In just a short time, you would lose consciousness, and your physical body would "overrule" your spirit/soul. So then, we see that your conscious mind has some degree of authority over your body, but your physical body has some degree of control over your conscious decisions.

The fact is that many things about your life are decided at the level of your body, and you do not have the will-power in your soul/spirit to overpower them. This is true of many physical desires and needs, most of which you are not even conscious.

Decisions made within the body go beyond physical functions. Paul explained that the body actually is involved in moral decisions, and that the body may have within it the desire to sin:

> I find then the principle that evil is present in me, the one who wishes to do good. For I joyfully concur with the law of God in the inner man, but I see a different law in the members of my body, waging war against the law of my mind, and making me a prisoner of the law of sin which is in my members. Wretched man that I am! Who will set me free from the body of this death? (Rom. 7:21-24).

Notice that the will is located in both the inner man and in the body. In the experience Paul described in these verses, the will of the body is greater than the will of the inner man. We must conclude, then, that the will of a man — to sin or not to sin — is, in part, located within his physical body.

We want you to realize that in some cases the body actually can have greater force to control a human being than the soul and the spirit. Just think about a person who has been injected with certain drugs. Many drugs are so powerful that a person can be controlled totally by them in his thoughts and actions. This shows us that the soul/spirit does not have a free will completely independent of the body.

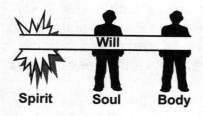

In discussing the will located within the body, we have mentioned the struggle between the inner man and the outer man. This carries with it the assumption of the will in the spirit/soul. Most Christians readily would admit to the role the spirit/ soul plays in determining man's decisions and destiny. We, therefore, do not need to spend a lot of time proving the will's existence on the deeper levels, other than to point out the following.

We explained how the spirit gives a person the energy to live and think. If an individual does not have enough spiritual strength, he will be ruled by that lack and be incapable of acting in the way he desires.

It is enlightening for us also to see how God can influence people's decisions through their spirit. For example, we read how "...the Lord stirred up the spirit of Cyrus the king of Persia..." (Ezra 1:1). Consider also the words of Isaiah spoken to those under God's judgment:

> For the Lord has poured over
> you a spirit of deep sleep,
> He has shut your eyes... (Isaiah
> 29:10)

The people under such a spiritual influence were incapable of seeing (see also Rom. 11:8). They had no free will to act independently of the spiritual influence enveloping them.

From the evil side, we could talk about how devils may tempt or "inspire" a person to make certain decisions. An evil spirit may have such a hold on a person's life that his behavior actually is controlled.

In later chapters we will explain some other truths, showing how spiritual influences determine who you are and how you act. Let's go on here to consider the soul. Many decisions are made at this level.

First, consider God's nature, since several verses in the Bible tell of the decisions He makes from within His soul. Most of these have to do with value judgments, and the acceptance or rejection of certain things:

> 'Moreover, I will make My dwelling among you, and My soul will not reject you' (Lev. 26:11).

> '...My soul shall abhor you' (Lev. 26:30).

> "But I will raise up for Myself a faithful priest who will do according to what is in My heart and My soul..." (I Sam. 2:35).

In the above verses, we are emphasizing decisions and judgments God makes from within His soul. This has a correlation to man's nature, because we believe God created man in His own image. Man has a free will to some degree and, as God decides from within His soul to reject or accept certain things, so does man.

To see that the soul can exercise authority over the spirit, we can refer to two verses which show it to us clearly:

> Like a city that is broken into
> and without walls
> Is a man who has no control
> over his spirit (Prov. 25:28).

> and the spirits of the prophets
> are subject to the prophets
> (I Cor. 14:32).

Notice that a person can exercise authority over his spirit. (In Volume III, Chapter 6, we explain when and why this is necessary).

Our main point in all this is to show how man's free will is not a completely independent agent, located at some specific point within his being. Teachings that try to position the free will of man only within the soul, only within the body, or only within the spirit, are an oversimplification and Biblically wrong.

Consider one example here which makes this truth obvious. Clarence is a man who gave himself over to a homosexual lifestyle for many years before becoming a Christian. As he repeatedly and continually submitted himself to sinful behaviors, his entire being became conformed to the related desires and thoughts. Because of evil lusts, Clarence drew within himself the spiritual influences related to that perversion. His spirit was defiled and submitted to the homosexual culture and demonically inspired habits. Over the course of time, his physical body developed cravings for that type of sexual satisfaction. His soul became bonded to another man and actually conformed to the thoughts and desires related to the homosexual lifestyle. The desires and the will for those homosexual tendencies permeated his entire being.

The Breath of God in Us

When Clarence became a Christian, freedom came only after a cleansing of his entire being. He repented and asked God to forgive him; however, his body continued to crave unnatural sexual pleasures for a time. He had many thought patterns that he had to renew according to God's Word and God's desires. Even though he was no longer taking part in the evil behavior, Clarence still had a feminine tone in his voice, and he unconsciously made gestures associated with that perverted lifestyle. He did not become entirely free until there had been a rejection of the evil influences — spirit, soul, and body.

We could talk about any obvious sin and see its influence throughout man's entire being. Since the will of man exists throughout his entire being, the Apostle Paul prayed for the early Christians, saying,

> Now may the God of peace
> Himself sanctify you entirely;
> and may your spirit and soul
> and body be preserved
> complete... (I Thess. 5:23).

A prayer such as this for sanctification only makes sense if our entire being is involved in sin. What we see then, is that the will of man involves and permeates his whole being.

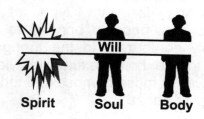

Closely related to this is the fact that man's heart exists on all three levels. To see this, we must grasp the bigger picture of how God created man. Realize that man is a whole person, not divided into three parts. The soul fills the body. The spirit fills the soul. All three parts are intermeshed and superimposed one upon the other. What the body has, the soul has. What the soul has, the spirit has. The various parts of our nature were not fashioned by different makers. No. God created all three parts after the same image. They fit together in one package.

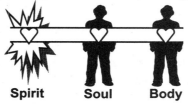

Spirit   Soul   Body

It is most accurate if we see the body as the physical expression of our invisible existence. The body has a heart. Therefore, the soul and spirit have a heart.

We can identify the heart at all three levels by looking at our own bodies and by examining certain Scriptures. First, we know that a medical doctor can cut a person open and see a physical organ, which we call the heart, pumping blood. However, the Bible talks about a heart at deeper levels. For example, when a person becomes a Christian, Jesus comes to dwell in his heart. Galatians 4:6 says:

> And because you are sons,
> God has sent forth the Spirit of
> His Son into our hearts, crying,
> "Abba! Father!"

Notice where Jesus dwells in the Christian's being —
in his heart. We do not see this on the physical level
and conclude that our Lord abides in the physical
organ; otherwise, people who have heart transplants
in our hospitals would be receiving Jesus every time
the newly implanted heart was from a Christian.
Obviously, we are not talking about the heart within
the natural body.

In locating the heart, we must see it as existing
throughout the core of man's being. The Greek word
for heart, *kardia*, also means the core or the very
center. In our everyday conversation, we can talk
about the heart of an issue, or the core of a specific
item, such as the core of an apple. It is in this sense
that we also can talk about the heart of man being at
his deepest center. At the center of his body is the
heart; at the center of his soul is also his heart; and
finally at the core of man's spirit is also his heart.

Spirit/Soul/Body

What then is the heart? It is the seat of desires
(Matt. 5:28), faith (Rom. 10:10), and purpose (Acts
11:23; II Cor. 9:7). We also know that it is the
fountainhead of man's life. Proverbs 4:23 tells us:

> Watch over your heart with all
> diligence,
> For from it flow the springs of
> life.

This truth, which also is revealed in other Bible passages, shows us the heart as the focal point of our being. Just as the physical heart pumps blood, so also the heart within our spirit/soul circulates the springs of life. The physical heart draws in oxygen through the lungs and food from the stomach. In a corresponding way, the invisible heart draws in evil through lusts and good through holy desires (Volume I, Chapter 9). That which is received grows and flows outward. The heart then is the core of man's being, while at the same time serving as the *fountainhead of life*.

Spirit/Soul/Body

This point cannot be emphasized enough for our future understanding. Wherever the heart of a man is pointed, his life will follow. From the heart of man, do, indeed, flow the springs of life.

Finally, let us put together the overall picture we have developed of man's nature. In our attempt to see man as a whole person, we have dispelled the misconceptions of people who held that the various functions of man are limited to only the spirit, soul, or body. Earlier, we saw how man's emotions and thought processes involve the entire person. Now, we are seeing how the heart and will also exist throughout his being.

God's Spirit
and the Christian's Spirit

In the life of the Christian there is an amiable relationship established between God's Spirit and the believer's spirit. When we refer to God's Spirit, we are speaking of the Holy Spirit. The two are the same. It is the relationship between the Holy Spirit and the Christian's spirit which we need to discuss.

Holy Spirit

Christian

Spirit   **Soul**   **Body**

The Christian's spirit, even though it is born of God, is still an entity separate from the Holy Spirit. Romans 8:16 tells us:

> The Spirit Himself bears wit-
> ness with our spirit that we are
> children of God.

The Breath of God in Us

Notice that there is an agreement between the Holy Spirit and the spirit within the born-again Christian, but they are still distinct entities.

This distinction can be identified when we discuss how the Christian's spirit is subject to the Christian, as Paul wrote:

> and the spirits of prophets are subject to prophets (I Cor. 14:32).

The Christian can exercise authority over his own spirit. In contrast, we know that the Holy Spirit is always subject to God the Father (John 16:13-15).

When a person becomes a Christian, he becomes a temple for the Holy Spirit to indwell (I Cor. 6:19). The Christian, therefore, has both his own spirit and the Holy Spirit present within.

We must not think of the entirety of the Holy Spirit dwelling within the Christian. To state this simply: "God is big!" When the Jews in the Old Testament times started to think that God was dwelling exclusively within their temple, God declared from heaven that the earth is His footstool (Is. 66:1). It is true that God's presence manifested at times in the Jewish temple, but not "all of God" was contained within it.

We also can learn from a passage in Malachi 2, where we see God rebuking people who broke their marriage covenants, declaring that none of them have a "remnant" or a "residue" of the Spirit left (Mal. 2:15). Such terminology implies that the measure of the Spirit within a person can change.

Only Jesus Christ had the complete fullness of the Spirit while on this earth. We, as Christians, have the first fruits (Rom. 8:23), or the down payment of His fullness (II Cor. 1:21-22).

What we must recognize is that the Holy Spirit is not a force or impersonal power. He is a Person. He can be grieved (Eph. 4:30) or quenched (I Thess. 5:19). God the Father is jealous over the Holy Spirit:

> Or do you think that the Scripture speaks to no purpose: "He jealously desires the Spirit which He has made to dwell in us"? (James 4:5).

In the context of this verse, James proceeds to say that as we draw near to God, He draws near to us. It is true that God will not abandon us; but it is also true that He fills our temple and reveals Himself to us in various ways, depending upon our heart attitude toward Him. He even is jealous over the Holy Spirit, and He will not allow the presence of the Spirit to fill an unholy temple.

On the other hand, as the Christian yields his life to the Father, the Holy Spirit takes more and more control of his life. Paul wrote:

> But the one who joins himself to the Lord is one spirit with Him (I Cor. 6:17).

The context of this verse is making a comparison with two people who are having sexual relations. As two become one, through bonding in sexual intercourse, so also the Holy Spirit and the Christian's spirit become one as the Christian joins himself to the Lord.

Notice that this understanding portrays the Christian's spirit as *not* always one with the Holy Spirit. The relationship between the Holy Spirit and the Christian's spirit changes from time to time.

Compare the relationship with a marriage. Two people who are married live together, have a bond between them, and have a covenant relationship. However, they may not be in total agreement and unity at one specific moment. At other times, they may be in harmony as their hearts agree with one another. At that time they are "one" in a much deeper sense of the word.

In similar fashion, we understand that the Christian's spirit and the Holy Spirit are bonded, and exist in the same dimension; and that there is a covenant relationship which God has established. It is as the believer yields his will to the Lord, that the Holy Spirit and the Christian's spirit "become one." This oneness is not automatic; otherwise, the Apostle Paul would not have exhorted the Corinthian Christians to "join" themselves to the Lord. If we were always one with Him, it would be wrong for James to tell us that as we draw near to Him, He draws near to us (James 4:5). Such exhortations can only be understood as we understand that the Holy Spirit is a Person, separate from the Christian's spirit, yet willing to unite as we fully yield to Him.

No Christian remains completely one with God every day of his life. We all fail and choose in our hearts to go our own ways. Until we see Him in glory, we always will struggle with our own wills. As we pointed out earlier, what we have at this stage of our lives is the first fruits of the Spirit (Rom. 8:23) and the down payment of His fullness (II Cor. 1:21-22).

If we think of God's Spirit as His breath and man's spirit as the residue of God's breath in us, we can make a powerful illustration here. One group of people on the North American continent express their love for each other, not by kissing each other, but by standing very close to each other and inhaling each other's breath. This symbolizes an exchange of life between them. In similar fashion, God draws near to His people and there is an exchange of spiritual substance, Spirit to spirit.

The Greek word used in the original Bible writings and interpreted *inspire*, literally means *to breath into*. When we speak of God inspiring something, we are saying that God has breathed in His life, energy, thoughts, authority, and/or nature.

Keep in mind at this point that man is a whole person. God does not merely breathe into the spirit of the Christian without influencing the soul and body. As we have emphasized, it is impossible to touch the spirit without touching the soul and the body at the same time. In fact, the Bible emphasizes that the Christian's *body* is the *temple* in which the Spirit dwells (I Cor. 3:16-17). It is impossible to have more of God's Spirit in the Christian's spirit than in the Christian's body. The spirit and the body are intermeshed and cannot be separated. The same can be said of the soul. To whatever degree God's Spirit is filling the Christian's spirit, it has to be filling the Christian's soul. The spirit, soul, and body are not separate packages. Man is a whole person, and as the Spirit of God fills him, his entire being is changed.

A Temple for the Holy Spirit

Becoming completely one with God - this should be our goal as Christians. Jesus was able to say, "I and the Father are one" (John 10:30). His will and the Father's will were in perfect harmony. Our Lord prayed for us, saying.

> "that they may all be one; even as Thou, Father, art in Me, and I in Thee, that they also may be in Us...." (John 17:21).

We have not yet attained to this perfect oneness with each other, nor with the Father, but we are "being transformed into the same image from glory to glory" (II Cor. 3:18). We are progressing toward to that goal.

We must understand that in this process, the union of the Holy Spirit and the Christian's spirit is not just a *mixing* of two entities; rather they "become one." The believer's spirit then becomes inseparable from the Holy Spirit. They are indistinguishable. We no longer then can talk about the Christian's spirit and the Holy Spirit as separate entities. Consider Paul's words again:

> But the one who joins himself to the Lord *is one spirit* with Him (I Cor. 6:17 — emphasis added).

When a Christian's will is in total union with God's will, then their spirits are no longer two, but are made into one entity.

Consider the implications of this. When the Christian, who is one with the Father, releases the human spirit within him, he also is releasing the Holy Spirit to flow out. When he yields to the spiritual urging within, he is yielding to God. When words come out of his mouth, they are the words of God. When he uses his authority, he is using God's authority. If, indeed, a Christian was totally one with the Father, his spirit, his words, his thoughts, and his authority would be God's Spirit, words, thoughts, and authority.

Sometime people will ask, "Are we releasing the Holy Spirit or the human spirit?" If a Christian's heart is in harmony with God's heart, then the Holy Spirit and his spirit are one; therefore, to release the human spirit is to release the Holy Spirit.

In contrast, when a person is not in submission to God, he may release his own spirit separate from the Holy Spirit. In the Old Testament, we read the warning concerning prophets who prophesy from their own inspiration and their own spirit, rather than from the Spirit of God (Ezek. 13:2-3). Jesus explained that he who seeks his own glory speaks from himself (John 7:18). Notice that the heart of a person determines what spirit is motivating him.

When a Christian desires to please God in all that he does, then the Holy Spirit will come and join with his spirit to the extent that the two are no longer two but one.

Apply this truth to various ministry situations. Many Christians wonder how they can see God's glory manifest in the world and in the midst of the Church. The answer is to become one with God and release that which is within them. If a certain minister desires to release the Spirit of God as he preaches, then he must release the human spirit which is within him. If a worship leader wants the presence of God to manifest in the midst of the congregation, he must let his own spirit fill the building. When a Christian desires to release healing power for the physically ill, he must release the spirit abiding within. If Christians hesitate in releasing the spirit within them, then they are holding back the workings of the Holy Spirit of God. To the degree they allow a free flowing of the spiritual energy within them, to that same degree they are releasing the Spirit of God, which is one with their spirit.

Dr. David Yonggi Cho, who at the time of this writing heads up the largest church in the world, has an interesting teaching which we can mention at this point. When asked by the pastors under his care how they could bring the presence of God to their meetings, he once responded by saying, "You bring His presence by your words." This is a profound statement, because it implies that releasing or bringing in the presence of God is dependent upon us and what we do.

Jesus said that we have the authority to bind or loose. The Holy Spirit, He said, would flow from *our* innermost being (John 7:37-39). Of course, God can and does move sovereignly by His Spirit in this world, but believers also must realize that the moving of God's Spirit is dependent upon our willingness to release the human spirit within our beings. Where our spirit goes, the Holy Spirit goes. Of course, this is only true to the extent that we have joined ourselves to the Lord.

This truth of our spirit being one with God's Spirit reveals one reason why the Holy Spirit flows out of people differently. Though we are one, we still have our individual personalities. God uses our unique personalities as He moves through our lives.

Compare this with the marriage relationship. When two people join in marriage and they are becoming one in heart, they maintain their distinct personalities. Though their desires melt together and complement one another, they still act as unique persons.

In similar fashion, the Christian does not lose his personality when he makes himself one with the Lord. Fleshly desires and selfish goals disappear, but personhood remains a part of what flows out. This is how our relationship with God works.

Finally, we need to add that even though our goal as Christians should be to be one with the Father, it is a serious error to lose sight of His distinct and separate existence from us. Sometime Christians, in learning about the Holy Spirit who dwells within, begin to focus all their attention upon that which God is doing in their own innermost being. Then they become confused about who God is. They start perceiving God as a force who moves within them, rather than as a Person separate from them. They live their lives waiting to yield to that which is within, and they often lose sight of a God who is in heaven. They may become confused concerning whether they should pray to God, or simply wait for Him to move within them. Only if we see God as a separate Person, greater than ourselves, will we have a proper relationship to Him. Even Jesus taught us to pray to the Father "who is in heaven." It is as we keep our minds focused upon a personal God above, that He becomes one with us within.

Compare again our relationship to the Father with a marriage relationship. When a husband focuses his heart and mind upon his wife, there arises within him desires and thoughts of how to please her. It is as they focus upon one another that they become one. In the same way, as the Christian turns his heart toward God, there rises from within him desires and thoughts concerning how to please God. As we focus upon God, He becomes one in spirit with us.

What we want you to see is that the focus for Christians should be upon God the Father Who is in heaven, and Who is a separate Person from themselves. Nowhere in the Bible are we told to focus upon the human spirit within, but many Bible verses exhort us to set our minds upon God who is in heaven. Colossians 3:1-2, for example tells us to:

> ...keep seeking the things above, where Christ is, seated at the right hand of God. Set your mind on the things above, not on the things that are on earth.

Even though God comes to dwell within the believer, our focus is not to be inward — but upward. The inward indwelling is the result.

This point is important.

One of our goals is to learn the functions of man's spirit. Thus far we have seen that the spirit gives us life and it enables us to think. It energizes our being. It is also the part of our nature with which God makes

Himself one. As a Christian becomes one with the Lord, his entire soul and body become saturated with God's Spirit, and he becomes a temple in which God dwells. With this under-standing, we can move on in our discovery of the nature of man and how he relates to the spiritual world.

Can Evil Reside Within a Christian?

Can evil spiritual substance be inside a Christian who has a spirit made alive by God? Can both good and evil exist within the same vessel?

To answer this, first of all consider what happened to the Apostle Peter. In Matthew 16:16, we read how Peter spoke his great confession of faith to our Lord: "Thou are the Christ, the Son of the living God." Jesus then responded to Peter, explaining that only God could have revealed this to him. However, just six verses later, we read how Peter pulled Jesus aside and rebuked Him. Jesus then responded to Peter, saying, "Get behind Me, Satan! You are a stumbling block to Me; for you are not setting your mind on God's interests, but man's" (Matt. 16:23b). Notice how the first statement Peter made was inspired by God; the second — focusing on human interests — was inspired by the devil.

God

The Breath of God in Us

Every Christian could give examples of how they have had to choose between God's thoughts and Satan's temptations. We already have discussed how God breathes into the Christian. We also know that Satan has the power to tempt us, which is his ability to inspire thoughts and desires.

In James 1:14-15, we are told more about what actually happens when we are tempted:

> But each one is tempted when he is carried away and enticed by his own lust. Then when lust has conceived, it gives birth to sin; and when sin is accomplished, it brings forth death.

Notice that people — even Christians — can lust; that is, turn their hearts and then desire things from an evil motivation. That lust actually *conceives* the evil within. By using this terminology, a comparison is being made with how a woman conceives a child within her. In similar fashion, people draw within their own beings the evil which they desire. That evil enters like a seed, and over the course of time, it grows, eventually bringing forth sin.

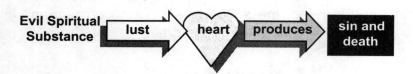

Not only is evil substance conceived within an individual, but every person also can bring evil thoughts into himself. Whenever a person submits to the devil's temptation, that individual is bringing the demonic thoughts into his own being. Recognizing these realities, we must conclude that evil spiritual influences can be brought into a person through his own desires and through the submission of his will.

This is true even in the life of the Christian. We must be careful to understand that the life of God is resident within the believer. Light and darkness oppose each other. Both good and evil spiritual substance can be within a single person, but the two must be seen as distinct in character.

The possibility of both good and evil spiritual substance being within a Christian is important to understand. Some Christians have a difficult time comprehending this, because they are thinking from a natural perspective of limited space. In Volume I, we explained how space has a different meaning in the spiritual dimension. We pointed out that a legion of devils, meaning at least a thousand devils, existed within a single person in the Bible (Luke 8:30). This implies that spiritual space is not limited, as we understand.

To see this even more clearly, we can ask the question, "Can the Holy Spirit and the devil be in the same region, such as a city, together?" The answer is obviously, "Yes." Can they be in the same building together? Yes, because the devil even came into the presence of Jesus to tempt Him (Matt. 4:3-11). Can they be in the same room together? Yes, because the book of Job describes how Satan goes into the very throne room of God (Job 1:6). Next, answer this: "Is there more space inside a room than there is inside a person's spirit?" There is no right answer to this question, because spiritual space has a meaning different from what we understand space to be in the natural.

To settle this whole issue of good and bad being in the same vessel, simply read the words of Paul in talking about his own struggles:

> I find then that evil is present in
> me, the one who wishes to do
> good (Rom. 7:21).

In the context of this verse, the Apostle Paul explained that evil dwelt within his body, while his inner man wanted to please God. Evil and good lodged in different places, however, both were present within his own being.

This conclusion is inescapable: the Christian can have evil spiritual substance within him.

This point is so critical for our later discussions, that we need to identify what actually happens within a person when he or she becomes a Christian, that is, becomes born again.

Through the work of Jesus Christ, people may find forgiveness of sin, and God does a cleansing work within them (Acts 15:9; Titus 3:5). God intervenes in the life of the individual, and breathes new spiritual life into the person who believes in Jesus. Once this new life has been introduced within the Christian's being, communion with God is restored, and a bond is created between God's Spirit and the Christian's spirit.

The significant point we need to make is that God has breathed new life into the believer. Hence, he is "born of God." Just as God first breathed life into Adam, He again breathes life into the believer. This life is new spiritual energy from God's nature. Through such a "born-again experience," he is made a member of a new family line, and the life of God flows into him through Jesus Christ.

There are some Christians today who teach that more happens through the born-again experience than what I just stated. They add that the entire spirit of the Christian is transformed, and the substance previously making the person's spirit is replaced by new substance. What they teach is that the Christian's entire spirit is instantly made perfect and re-created totally in the image and glory of God. They say that the spirit of the Christian cannot be corrupted, hurt, or improved upon in any way. This is the "perfect-spirit doctrine."

I disagree with that teaching and want to warn you about subtle, yet destructive, implications of the perfect-spirit doctrine. (Several errors will become obvious in Volume III). Throughout these writings, I will be teaching from the more commonly accepted view that, when we become saved, God plants new life into our spirits, as a seed, that must grow and come forth over the course of time (I Peter 1:23).

Jesus made a comparison between our first birth and our second birth when He said, "You must be born again" (John 3:7). When we are born naturally of our parents, we are infants and must grow to maturity. It is with this same comparison that we understand the second birth. Though we are born of God, we are not fully mature immediately.

The Bible teaches us that we are "being transformed into the same image [of God] from glory to glory..." (II Cor. 3:18). It is not an instantaneous work of perfection which is accomplished at the new

55

birth; rather, a progressive one begins at that time. Once a person has been begotten of God, he progressively matures into a greater and greater manifestation of God's nature, as he yields to the ongoing work of the Holy Spirit. Jesus, indeed, does dwell by the Spirit in the Christian's spirit, but the believer's spirit is not yet perfect.

Those who teach that the Christian's entire spirit is instantaneously perfect misinterpret two verses from the Bible in order to justify their doctrinal position. In Hebrews 12:23, we can read a reference being made to "...the spirits of righteous men made perfect...." The perfect-spirit teachers like to include themselves in this description, but in reality, this phrase refers to those who have died and already are living in the presence of God. Furthermore, the verse tells us that those people who have died have been made perfect — not just their spirits, but they themselves have been made perfect. Yes, those now with Jesus have been transformed into His image, but we are not yet in that group.

The other verse that sometime is misinterpreted is the King James translation of Second Corinthians 5:17, which says:

> Therefore if any man be in Christ, he is a new creature: old things are passed away; behold, all things are become new.

Using this verse, the perfect-spirit teachers stress the word "all" and imply that all the Christian's spirit is made totally perfect.

I do not want to lessen the magnificence of what God has done through Jesus Christ, and how grateful we as believers must be; however, we need not "help" God by adding to the Scriptures.

Those who teach the perfect-spirit doctrine assume that the Apostle Paul was referring to the Christian's spirit when he said "all things." Yet the context of this verse in no way indicates that the things being made new refer to the spirit of the Christian. In reality, Paul is speaking of the change in our *relationship to God, our perspective of life, and how we live* — all these things have become new.

To see that Paul was not teaching the perfect-spirit doctrine in Second Corinthians 5:17, all one has to do is read 23 verses later where Paul went on to tell the Corinthian Christians:

> Therefore, having these promises, beloved, let us cleanse ourselves from all defilement of flesh and spirit, perfecting holiness in the fear of God (II Cor. 7:1).

The perfect-spirit teachers must block this verse out of their minds in order to continue holding to their doctrine. Since Paul talks in this verse about the Christian's spirit being *defiled* and *needing cleansing*, he obviously was not teaching 23 verses earlier that the Christian's spirit is already perfect.

It is important that we note that in the verse we just quoted, Paul was speaking to Christians: to *"beloved"* who *"have the promises of God."* He also includes himself in this exhortation: "let *us* cleanse *ourselves* of all defilement of flesh and spirit." Obviously, the Christian's spirit can be defiled.

Our perspective throughout these volumes is that God plants His seed within us when we put our faith in Jesus. That seed is incorruptible (I Peter 1:23). Our spirits are not perfect, but the seeds within our spirits are from the very substance of God, and therefore, perfect.

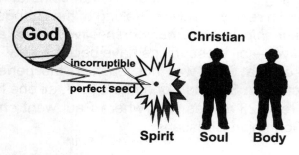

There are several Bible passages which contradict the perfect-spirit doctrine. This issue has so many far-reaching implications, and is so critical for topics which will follow, that it is worth our time to glance at a few verses which verify this.

For example, we must take into account Paul's exhortations in the New Testament for Christians to stay "in one spirit," that is in Greek, *en heis pneumatos* (Phil. 1:27; see also Eph. 4:3). If Christians already had a perfect spirit, they always would be perfectly united in spirit, and Paul's exhortation would be foolish and wrong. That would be like telling a person, "Do not sin," while at the same time believing that they *could not* sin. The obvious point is that Christians *can* sin and they *can* be spiritually disunited.

Several Bible verses also talk about things being added to the Christian's spirit. For example, Paul wrote to the Philippians:

> The grace of the Lord Jesus Christ be with your spirit (Phil. 4:23).

Paul ended his letter to the Galatians with the same words (Gal. 6:18). He also used this exhortation in his letter to Philemon (Philemon 1:25). The idea that nothing can be added to the Christian's spirit is contrary to Biblical truth.

Paul ended the Second Letter to Timothy with these words:

> The Lord be with your spirit. Grace be with you (II Tim. 4:22).

Such a salutation would be wrong if the Christian's spirit was perfect and already in perfect unity with Jesus Christ.

Peter exhorted the Christian women to have "a gentle and quiet spirit" (I Peter 3:4), a teaching which would be foolish if the Christian's spirit was perfect. In Romans 12:11, Paul exhorted all believers to serve the Lord, being "fervent in spirit." Similarly, he commanded the unmarried women to dedicate themselves to the Lord that they "may be holy both in body and spirit" (I Cor. 7:34). Such terminology would be in error if the Christian's spirit was perfect in holiness simply because of the new-birth experience.

The Breath of God in Us

In Second Corinthians 7:13, we read Paul's words to the Corinthians concerning Titus:

> ...because his spirit has been refreshed by you all.

A perfect spirit would not need refreshing, and it would have been wrong for Paul to speak in these terms, if, indeed, the Christian's spirit was already perfect.

More than one Bible passage refers to a broken, crushed, or wounded spirit, for example:

> The spirit of a man can endure his sickness,
> But a broken spirit who can bear? (Prov. 18:14).

> A soothing tongue is a tree of life,
> But perversion in it crushes the spirit (Prov. 15:4).

> A joyful heart is good medicine,
> But a broken spirit dries up the bones (Prov. 17:22).

King David often spoke of pressures to which his spirit was subjected. Consider the following:

> When my spirit was overwhelmed within me... (Ps. 142:3).

> Answer me quickly, O LORD,
> my spirit fails... (Ps. 143:7).
>
> Therefore my spirit is over-
> whelmed... (Ps 143:4).

Other references talk about being "oppressed in spirit" (i.e., I Sam. 1:15). Isaiah prophesied:

> "Then the spirit of the Egyp-
> tians will be demoralized within
> them" (Is. 19:3a).

Such Scripture passages which refer to negative effects upon the spirit of man are numerous.

Although the references in the previous paragraph are taken from the Old Testament, the ten verses which I gave you preceding those all are recorded in the New Testament, and all ten of them are speaking about Christians. In the Old Testament, numerous verses talk about a person's spirit being broken, crushed, bruised, overwhelmed, failing, demoralized, etc. In the New Testament several verses discuss the Christian's spirit being defiled, refreshed, having grace added to it, being in unity or disunity with other believers, etc.

In Romans 8:10, we are told that the Christian's spirit is "alive because of righteousness." Because the seed of righteousness has been planted within, the spirit of the believer, indeed, is alive. The term *alive* is not a synonym for the word *perfect*. We understand that the spirit is alive unto God; that is, responsive to Him, and now open to grow into His likeness.

The Breath of God in Us

The Bible clearly shows us that even the Christian can be subject to negative spiritual influences. For example, Paul had to exhort Timothy not to yield to a "spirit of timidity" (II Tim. 1:7). In Second Corinthians 11:4, he told the Christians not to receive a spirit contrary to the gospel. And then, of course, Paul exhorted all Christians to "be renewed in the spirit of your mind," which implies that the spirit of their mind at times can be bad (Eph. 4:23).

Some people may want to interpret these last three verses merely as figures of speech and deny that negative spiritual influences actually can enter into the Christian. They may try to explain them away by saying that evil spiritual substance actually does not enter the spirit of the Christian. I choose not to explain these Scriptures away, nor excuse them as figures of speech. There are times that Christians can receive within themselves a spirit of timidity, a spirit contrary to the gospel, and/or negative spiritual influences upon their mind. Whether or not that evil substance is in the Christian's spirit, we must recognize that evil spiritual substance can be somewhere within the Christian's being.

Let me repeat that: Both good and evil spiritual entities or substance can be in the same place at the same time. We know that Satan himself came right into the presence of Jesus Christ in order to test Him in the wilderness (Matt.4:1-11). In the Book of Job we find that Satan came into the very throne room of God to talk to God Himself (Job 1:6). The Apostle Paul recognized that sin dwelt within him, even though he was a Christian (Rom. 7:21). All people conceive evil through their own lusts. Other Bible verses declare this, as well. Therefore, we must conclude that evil and good may exist in the same place, even in the same human vessel.

It is our belief that within a Christian, good and evil substance can dwell. The Word of God may be growing within a person and at the same time the devil can come and sow tares which grow up to produce bad fruit (Matt. 13:25). The substance of this good and bad is not natural, but spiritual in nature. Yes, spiritual substance, good or bad, can be within the believer.

Only if we accept this truth can we understand Paul's words to the Corinthian Christians, "...let us cleanse ourselves from all defilement of flesh and spirit..." (II Cor. 7:1). Since Paul included himself in this exhortation, we must include ourselves. These are not words to be denied, but embraced and understood.

It will help for our future discussions to under-stand how this defilement of spirit can happen. In the context of Second Corinthians 7:1, Paul was cautioning the early Christians not to be bound together with unbelievers, especially with those who are lawless and who worship idols (II Cor. 6:14-17). From this context, we conclude that a Christian's spirit can become defiled through close relationships with evil people.

We can read this same warning in other pas-sages, such as where Paul instructed the early Christians to expel a certain sexually perverted man from their midst, because "a little leaven leavens the whole lump of dough" (I Cor. 5:6). Evil spiritual influences do indeed spread, even among Christians.

The Breath of God in Us

In Volume IV, we will go into detail concerning how evil spiritual substance may be passed from one person to another. If you want to learn more about this topic, I refer you to that discussion. For now, let us heed Paul's warning of how a Christian's spirit may be defiled. It may occur as the result of bonding with unbelievers involved with evil. It also may be the result of the Christian himself lusting after evil influences and/or submitting to Satan's will.

7

The Spiritual Side to Physical Health

With the information which we have gained thus far, we now want to consider the physical body and see how physical health is influenced by all that is going on in the spirit, soul, and body.

First of all, we must answer the fundamental question, "What is life?" We have explained that all life originated from God. If we were to talk about animal or plant life, we would point to its source as the supernatural power within God's spoken words at Creation. Sustaining man's existence, we see the breath God originally released into Adam, and we can identify how the spiritual substance of life is passed on through the generational lines. That spiritual substance abides within all people, enabling them to live. Life, then, is not just the biochemical or physiological activity within an organism. No. Life includes that, but it is more. *Life is the invisible energy resident within a creature and the resulting effect it has of activating that creature.*

If we truly accept this truth and consider its implications, it will challenge the very foundation of much modern-day thinking. Western scientific thought too often limits its focus to the physical existence of man. Medical studies, for example, include the examination of diseases, the activities of bacteria and viruses, the functions of the physical body, and the effects of various chemical and surgical treatments. These endeavors usually are restricted to natural cause-and-effect relationships, denying the spiritual side to man's makeup.

Traditional Western Thought:

Natural things----->cause-------->natural effects

Please do not take me wrong here. I am grateful for every advancement in medicine, and we as Christians should thank God for those giving their lives in order to help others who suffer from various diseases, illnesses, and pain. I do not want to sound critical in any way.

All we want to do here is open to a broader, more Biblical view of man's existence.

When I say that traditional medical studies have tended to deny the spiritual side to man's makeup, I am not judging them as being atheistic. No. Many scientists are devout Christians, and thousands of doctors today unite prayer and faith in God with their labors. Many are very spiritual men and women, and they are serving God to the best of their abilities.

What we mean here, by saying that traditional medicine tends to deny the spiritual side of man's existence, is this: Western thought has focused upon the natural world, and in relationship to medicine, upon the functions of the physical body. It does not fully recognize the existence of man's spirit/soul and its role in sustaining life. As Christians, we believe that man has a spiritual side to his being. Therefore, medicine could be much more effective today if man were examined and treated as a whole person.

We are speaking about more than the consideration of how people's emotional life and thought patterns affect their physical bodies. Most people will admit to the influence that emotional conditions such as worry, fear, bitterness, etc., can have upon the physical body. However, they usually are limiting their thinking to how biochemical reactions and dysfunctions in the body may be associated with emotions and thought patterns. Obviously, there is truth to that understanding. But in their minds, they typically are thinking of emotions and thought processes as being naturally-based elements. Therefore, they are considering merely cause-and-effect relationships, where natural things (biochemical reactions) are affecting other natural things (physical health).

Natural things-------->cause------>natural effects
Emotions & thoughts-->influence--->bodily health

Think deeper. Think bigger. It is the spirit which gives life. Both the soul and the spirit can and do influence the physical body. Something which is totally invisible, and which does not exist in this realm, can and does influence the physical body. Obviously, biochemical reactions and certain physiological changes occur, but these may be reactions in the natural to that which is happening in the spiritual. Therefore, Christians who are developing a Biblical view of man must ask the question, "What spiritual things are causing natural effects?"

Spiritual things------>cause--------->natural effects

To see this principle in the Bible, first read the words of James:

> Therefore, confess your sins to one another, and pray for one another, so that you may be healed (James 5:16a).

Then examine King David's words:

> When I kept silent about my sin, my body wasted away... (Ps. 32:3).

From many such verses, we have to conclude that the condition of one's spirit/soul will influence the condition of his physical body.

Spiritual things------>cause--------->natural effects
Spirit/soul --------->influences----->bodily health

We must consider not only the conditions within a person's spiritual side, but also the forces outside of us that are active in the spiritual dimension. For example, God has promised long life to those who honor their parents (Eph. 6:1-3 and Ex 20:12). Words spoken by God, such as these, establish spiritual forces which, indeed, do influence us.

Spiritual things----->cause-------->natural effects
Spiritual forces----->influence------>bodily health

We must go one step farther and add the active influence of spirit beings: God and devils. Consider this testimony from the ministry of Jesus:

> And behold, there was a woman who for eighteen years had had a sickness caused by a spirit; and she was bent double, and could not straighten up at all. And when Jesus saw her, He called her over and said to her, "Woman, you are freed from your sickness." And He laid His hands upon her; and immediately she was made erect again, and began glorifying God (Luke 13:11-13).

Notice that both God's and Satan's activities are involved with physical health.

Spiritual things----->influence------>natural effects
Spirit beings-------->influence------>bodily health

We are not saying that all sickness is caused by sin, spiritual forces, devils or spiritual entities. Please do not misunderstand this. We simply are pointing out the Biblical view, that spiritual things can and do influence natural things.

Notice that by taking this perspective we are not getting away from true science. *Science is the attempt to discover truth by observing evidence which can be tested and proven.* This is good. Christians must not be afraid of verifying truth. However, we also must realize that the effects of spiritual things and their role in physical health can be observed and tested today.

Compare this with how science has accepted the existence of gravity. Gravity never has been seen nor fully understood by scientists. All that the best scientists in the world have ever seen are the *effects of gravity.* No one ever has seen gravity itself, yet it is scientifically correct to accept the existence of gravity and to continue studying it. In the same way, it would be true scientifically to accept the existence of a spiritual side to man's existence, as long as we can see its effects upon the natural existence of man.

Unfortunately, many have equated Christianity with the Western, naturally-focused mind-set. Others have limited their thinking to natural cause-and-effect relationships, believing in error that they are being scientific. In reality, the narrow-minded pattern of Western thinking is neither scientific nor Christian. In fact, it is wrong — from a truly Christian perspective — to deal with man as merely a physical being.

The view of man and health which I am recommending here is more than what is called *holistic medicine* today. The term *holistic medicine* is used to describe a broader view of health than traditional medicine holds. Those involved in holistic practices focus much more on nutritious diets, the influence of emotions and thought patterns, the importance of faith, etc. Holistic medicine includes a wide range of practices, including biochemical feedback, acupuncture, meditation, reflexology, homeopathy, etc. There are an endless number of practices being investigated and used by those in holistic medicine.

We are not recommending these practices, nor condemning them. We will define a few in the next chapter and discuss how a Christian should view them. What we are attempting to do here is to lay a foundation for a Biblical, Christian perspective in regard to the whole issue of health. What we must declare at this point is that the true Christian view must be bigger than the traditional view of medicine, and even bigger than holistic medicine.

People involved in holistic medicine typically think they are broad-minded and getting the "whole view," but please recognize that even holistic medicine is limited. For example, when someone talks about biofeedback, they are referring to thought processes that influence the physical body. It is true that when you think positively you release bio-chemical reactions which are more beneficial to your health. However, do not make the mistake of thinking that biofeedback deals with the whole man. Most studies done in biofeedback limit their concept of thought processes to the natural processes within the human brain. They still are talking about natural cause-and-effect relationships, denying man's existence as a spirit/soul/body creature.

Similarly, we can talk about reflexology. This is the practice of massaging the patient's feet in particular ways, which are thought to activate certain bodily functions. Obviously, this is beyond traditional medical practices, but still they are limiting their understanding to natural causes producing natural effects.

When people refer to nutritious diets as being a form of holistic medicine, they still are thinking on the natural plane. Even when various teas and natural herbs are used by individuals for treatments of various illnesses, they are limiting themselves to the Western mind-set.

Again, let me say that the true Christian perspective must be broader minded, thereby including the spiritual as well as the natural.

Some people involved in holistic practices will go so far as to investigate *spiritual energies* within the human body. People in the Orient more commonly recognize the existence of these invisible energies. Many of those involved in New Age practices accept the related concepts and talk about balancing or releasing energies within.

As Christians, attempting to develop a Biblical perspective, we can give them credit for acknowledging the life energies within people. However, even *they* tend to limit their thinking by not being open to the *whole world of the spirit*. They still are focusing on something resident within man's body — invisible, but still located within. There is more than energy — there is a spirit and soul — plus a whole spiritual world in which we live. Also, they err in not recognizing evil spirit entities in the spiritual world. New Agers, for the most part, embrace spiritual experiences without discernment of good from evil. This, we will see, opens the door for much confusion and trouble.

The Spiritual Side to Physical Health

What we are asking you to do is embrace a Biblical view of man and his existence:

1. You are a spirit/soul/body creature.
2. There is an invisible energy within you sustaining your life.
3. You exist in two worlds — the spiritual and the natural.
4. There are both good and bad influences in both worlds.
5. God has established spiritual forces which act upon all of mankind.

Yes, we need to understand natural cause-and-effect relationships; however, we must think bigger. We must step back from the narrow-minded view of man, which sees him merely as a body in this world. If we are going to understand health, we must begin with a more Biblical view. The "whole" view of man considers all of the following:

Spiritual world	Natural World
God	Diet
	Disease
Spiritual forces	Accidents
	Medicine
Devils	Surgery
Spirit/Soul	Body

Before we apply this whole perspective, allow me to clarify our position again. We are not rejecting traditional medicine. We are grateful for all the work and advances accomplished in the related fields.

Some spirit-oriented Christians may read these words and wrongly think that we are prescribing an *only spiritual approach* to health. They would think doctors and medicine should be avoided. We are not saying nor implying this in any way. Instead, we are embracing a *whole* view, and teaching that man must be treated as a *whole* person. Whatever the cause of physical illness, be it natural or spiritual, it should be addressed. Health is a product of the spiritual and natural worlds, and the way we live in both. We thank God for doctors and encourage all people to receive the best possible medical treatment available to them.

At the same time, we do not expect the average medical doctor to be the person responsible to treat the whole man. It is OK for them to be narrow and focused toward the natural side. An auto mechanic focuses on the repairs of automobiles and we do not expect him to also be a carpenter who fixes homes. In comparison there is nothing wrong with medical doctors specializing in the natural cause-and-effect relationships — that is their job. In fact by specializing they are likely to be of more benefit to us. However all Christians, medically trained or not, should recognize the bigger picture involved with issues of health.

8
Holistic Practices versus Biblical Healing

Using the "whole concept of man" which we have developed thus far, we now want to look at health and consider some of the healing practices used in today's world. This is not a medical textbook. Our goal is simply to form a proper Biblical perspective. Because the naturally-oriented view is so common, we want to add the spiritual dimension to healing here.

Before we proceed, there is a spiritual principle which we laid out in Volume I, Chapter 8, which we quickly must mention again: *Singleness of eye releases spiritual energy from within and opens the door to the spiritual realm.* Because we developed this concept fully in Volume I, let's simply review the words of Jesus which teach this truth:

> "The lamp of the body is the eye; if therefore your eye is clear, your whole body will be full of light. But if your eye is bad, your whole body will be full of darkness" (Matt. 6:22-23a).

The Breath of God in Us

In this Bible passage we saw the significance of having the right focus of one's attention, affections, faith, and entire heart. When a person is single of eye, spiritual light floods his physical body. Spiritual energy from within is released, and spiritual influences in the spiritual world may flow through the person so focused. We also learned in our previous discussion (Vol. I, Chapter 8), how that upon which a person fixes his eye becomes his master, and he, in a sense, bows to its spiritual influence. This Biblical principle has profound implications when speaking about healing.

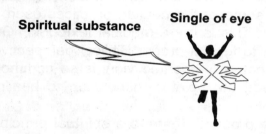

Spiritual substance   **Single of eye**

We now can see how some of the holistic healing techniques work today. Again, let me say that I am neither condoning nor condemning these. We simply are mentioning them for your understanding.

There are hundreds of different holistic practices, but our greatest interest here is with those involving *unseen energies*. Most, if not all, depend in some way upon the focusing of the patient's eye. We are not against such focusing, and, in fact, we will discuss how Christians should do this very thing. Our caution is based on the understanding that the focused eye not only allows one's own spiritual life to flow, but also opens the door for outside spiritual energies to enter.

Acupuncture, for example, is a method used to release the spirit-energies within the individual. Typically, sharp needles are inserted in sensitive areas on the human body. Related healing techniques have been used for centuries in the Orient and now are quickly spreading into the West.

The ancient practice of acupuncture is based on the premise that spiritual energies are flowing within the human body. Sickness, pain, and other ailments are thought to be the result of blockages or disruptions in the spiritual flow. They believe that tiny needles inserted in key pathways will stimulate or release normal healthy flows.

Again let me say, I neither am condoning nor condemning acupuncture; I am explaining it.

There are medical doctors today beginning to recommend or use acupuncture as a supplement to their traditional practices. Results cannot be denied. There are some verifiable positive effects.

Unfortunately, professionals in the West attempt to force their understanding of acupuncture into their Western framework. In attempting to explain why it sometime works, they immediately think in terms of electrical impulses or magnetic fields being released in the human body, rather than spiritual energies being released. Because they have their minds fixed on the natural cause-and-effect relationships, they have to try to find an explanation in the natural dimension.

As Christians, we need not do that! From the Biblical perspective, we accept the fact that there are spiritual energies flowing within every person. These God-given spirit-energies are essential for life and health. We should not accept all that the Oriental practitioners teach; however, we must accept the fundamental concept that man does have spiritual energies moving within.

Accepting this fact, how can we explain why acupuncture sometime works? We know that there are very few things in life which will focus the eye more singularly than a needle. The insertion of several needles in sensitive areas of the body causes the eye (that is, the focus of one's attention) to fixate. As we explained (Volume I, Chapter 4), pain tends to further make the individual detach from all other concerns in the natural world. The path for increased spiritual energy may then be opened, at least for a time, and the healing processes accelerated. We, as Bible-believing Christians, recognize that God created man with life-giving energy, and we see the need of activating it for the human body to function correctly.

However, our primary concern stems from energies which may move from the acupuncturist into the patient. In Chapter 6 we explained how bonding with people may lead to a defilement of spirit. If the patient has any measure of faith in the acupuncturist, he may submit his will to the practitioner's care and actually draw on the spiritual energy within him. Two spiritual energies then are activated: that which is within the spirit of the patient and that which flows through the one inserting needles. In many such healing methods, we see the patient becoming negatively influenced by the individuals doing the work. Very often the patient becomes more and more dependent upon the practitioner, finding temporary relief from one illness, but in a short time developing other sicknesses, which also demand the practitioner's services. The more people submit to a specific healing technique, the more they tend to admire, idolize, and even worship (in a sense) both the form of treatment they are receiving and the person administering it. Gradually, then, there comes an altering of the patient's beliefs and ways of thinking, as the practitioner's thoughts are impressed upon the person through a spiritual transfer.

(This discussion also carries with it warnings concerning our relationships with trusted doctors, counselors, dentists, teachers, ministers, etc., about which we will learn more in Volume IV).

There are many methods being promoted today which alter one's thought processes, including various forms of meditation, yoga, biofeedback techniques, and hypnotism. All of these alter the state of a person's mind and open the door for spiritual energies to flow. As Christians developing a Biblical understanding of spiritual dynamics, we can understand how some benefit may be obtained through the releasing of the spirit-energy resident within man. However, as we have been stressing, the focused, receptive soul also can be an open vessel to receive foreign spiritual energies.

The use of crystals is becoming more and more common in holistic healing today. Simply staring into a crystal can change the conscious state of an individual. Another use of the crystal is in the "balancing of a person's energies." One common way this is done is by suspending a crystal on a string, and then hypnotically swinging it back and forth over the body of the patient as he is lying down. The practitioner explains that the suspended crystal is made to swing out of alignment with the patient's body until the energies within the patient are freely flowing out.

Whether or not the path in which the crystal swings is indicative of "balance" within is debatable. However, even the Bible-believing Christian must recognize the importance of the spirit-energy flowing out. Relaxing and focusing upon a swinging crystal very well could release the God-given energies. Even though the crystal-swinging doctor may not give God the credit, it is God who designed us with a spirit that should be flowing from our innermost being. Again, we must caution the Christian against submitting his life to such care because the soul/spirit in such a relaxed, focused position is an open vessel for whatever evil energies are present at the time.

Crystals and other substances also are being used today in a way which creates a mystical belief in their power.

Homeopathy, for example, entails mixing tiny amounts of some substance in a fluid and then diluting the solution time and time again. They maintain that the more the solution is diluted, the more effective the "tincture" will be in helping the body resist diseases and various illnesses.

Using our whole concept of health and life, we can understand how tiny amounts of certain substances may influence the body. Our natural response mechanisms may be triggered in healthy ways much like vaccines often cause the body to develop specific immunities. However, we also must recognize that *some* homeopathic remedies depend upon a mystical belief in the diluted solutions. Many practitioners claim that the healing power is the result of unexplained energies within the solutions. A reverence often is created in the mind of the user. Those who practice homeopathy give various explanations for any positive effects produced, but it is our understanding that spiritual energy indeed can be released through the hope set upon the mysterious solution itself.

At this point we could bring light to an interesting side topic. We all have heard fairy tales of witches stirring their boiling pots of water, while adding their secret potions and hard-to-obtain articles such as lizard tails, the eye of a newt, the hair of a fair maiden, frog bones, etc. Anyone understanding spiritual principles knows that the magic power in their brew is not in the actual elements included, but in the mystical atmosphere created and spiritual energy released by people's hearts. The more secretive a potion is, and the harder it is to prepare, the more likely it is to captivate the onlooker's faith.

Now please do not think we are in any way recommending some witch's brew. Nor are we trying to equate today's homeopathic remedies to those dark, evil practices.

We simply are teaching the Biblical principle: *the single eye releases spiritual energy*.

We even see this, to some extent, in modern scientific studies today in what has been called the "placebo effect." Patients are given tablets containing nothing more than salt, sucrose, or some other noneffective chemical. Then they are told that the tablets are some powerful medicine that will relieve their pain or help cure their illness. In some cases, people involved in these experiments become healthier at an amazing rate. Having a Biblical view of man, we could explain this as the faith of the individual in action, but we also must point out that their faith had a focal point: either the tablets or the words of their doctor.

As Christians, we want to learn the proper place to focus our faith. How can we release the spiritual energies within our beings? Should we use placebos, homeopathic solutions, crystals, or the needles of the acupuncturist? On what should our faith rest?

Before we answer this, pay close attention to our understanding of faith here. It is the avenue by which we draw things from out of the spiritual realm and release them into the natural (Volume I, Chapter 9).

This view is very different from that held by the traditional Western mind. Many people in today's society will admit that faith plays a major role in the healing process, but their definition of faith includes nothing about releasing spiritual things into the natural world. When speaking of healing, they will encourage a sick person to "keep believing," by which they mean the patient should fix positive thoughts within their mind. They would admit that positive thoughts indeed can influence the body to function in certain ways, but they are envisioning the "tricking" of the physical body into healing itself by thinking good things rather than negative. Room may be left for God to work; however, the Western, scientific mind tends to see faith as a function of the brain or, at best, limited as a function of natural things causing natural effects.

Contrary to what the Western mind says, faith is not just a function of the brain. True faith is of the heart (Rom. 10:10). No trickery is involved. And when a person believes, he releases the spiritual energy within himself, and he opens his heart to actually draw in the substance of that which is in the spiritual realm.

False concept of faith:
Positive thoughts------>mind------->natural effects

Biblical concept of faith:
Spiritual substance---->heart------>natural effects

Then how can a Christian approach this whole area of healing and health with a Biblical perspective?

To begin, we can mention a general lifestyle and attitude which produces health. In addition to exercise and a good diet, we can discuss right-living before God. There are many promises in the Bible related to health — too many to mention here. We can say that having a holy, righteous reason to live can be more beneficial to health than the best medical treatment in the finest hospital. Getting priorities right can uncloud the mind and cause the physical body to function correctly. Cultivating a consistent joyful attitude can ward off illness. Simply having a concept of God being good and abundant produces a quality of life conducive to good health, in contrast to a view which sees God as mean and condemning (Matt. 6:25-34).

In addition to general lifestyles, we can talk about specific times set aside which are beneficial physically, emotionally — in all ways. For example, rest and relaxation were designed into God's original plan for mankind — to work six days each week and rest one. Quiet moments throughout a single day for prayer or Godly meditation can redirect a person's life and help him to be single of eye. When a person is sick, detaching from the innumerable concerns of one's life and focusing upon simple blessings can activate normal bodily functions. Listening to soothing music and sleeping can release healing. Whenever people simplify their lives and become single of focus, they will release the God-given healing power within them.

Also, the cleansing of the soul/spirit can help a sick person get well. The Bible tells us,

> Therefore, confess your sins to one another, and pray for one another, so that you may be healed (James 5:16).

Unconfessed sin can stop the proper functioning of the human body. When a person's being is contaminated with evil, sickness is a common mani-festation.

Now, we are not saying that every illness is the result of sin. No. There are injuries which are purely physical in nature; for example, when a person falls down and breaks his or her leg. There are diseases which we view as simply a part of the corrupted world in which we live. There are also diseases which are demonic in origin, as we can see from Scripture passages which tell about our Lord Jesus casting out "spirits of infirmity" (i.e., Matt. 8:16; Luke 13:11). In such cases, there may or may not be sin on the part of the afflicted individual. The devil attacks people as he did Job, and we are told in the Bible that he is always seeking someone to devour (I Peter 5:8). Therefore, sickness can be naturally or spiritually based, and the individual may or may not be responsible for it coming upon him.

Whatever the cause, the Bible-believing Christian believes in the healing power which can be released from within them. Also, we recognize the spiritual energy which can flow from one person into another, both positive or negative. On the positive side, having people love you will cause you to be healthier. A sick person can and does draw upon the strength of those around him. An individual who has been influenced negatively can be cleansed by ending detrimental relationships. In such cases there should be a renouncing of past involvement with the related evils and then a turning of one's heart toward God.

This cleansing work is important when we minister to someone who previously has been involved in certain holistic healing methods. Again, we say that not all holistic practices are bad, but we have seen, through experience, that many people, including Christians, have received negative spiritual influences within their being, by opening themselves up and yielding, without discerning the dangers involved. We have seen people experience healing in one particular area through holistic practices; however, it is very common for another sickness to appear, or a general deterioration in their health to occur. For example, one person may receive treatment for some allergy, but from that day on they are more susceptible to flu, colds, anemia, etc. We credit this deterioration to both the receiving of negative spiritual substance, and to the individual's bowing within their spirit to powers not of God. It is very common for people who get consumed in the entire holistic movement to have an overall decay in their health. In order for them to get free, they must renounce their involvement and turn their hope and faith toward God.

Similar deterioration in health can happen in Christian circles that become focused upon illnesses. For example, a church congregation may have several people become physically ill and so they begin to pray for them. Their prayers, however, are not ones of faith and victory. Instead, the people become focused on the illnesses. Every time they meet, they talk about who has cancer, who is in the hospital, and who is at home in bed. They think that they are being concerned and expressing love, but in reality they are becoming "single of eye" toward the power of illness. Soon it seems that a *spirit of illness* is moving throughout the congregation, and more and more people are touched by it. Such groups of Christians rarely break the curse of illness off themselves until they radically shift the focus of their attention and take on a whole different focus with their ministry.

A consistent poise of heart toward God, in thankfulness and rejoicing, releases healing power. Even when a person is under a doctor's care, or using certain medicines, he should keep his faith directed God-ward. This point of focus is dramatically seen in the testimony of the Jews who were bitten by serpents while wandering in the wilderness. God instructed Moses to raise up a staff, and those who fixed their eyes upon it were healed (Numbers 21:9). In that incident, healing power flowed from God; but setting their eyes and faith in a single direction opened the Jewish people to receive. Similarly, faith and singleness of heart opens a person to receive spiritual strength, even today.

Finally, in our discussion here we must not limit our thinking to the spiritual energy within people. We also are talking about the powers which flow from the spiritual realm. The Christian has access to the very nature of God and the healing touch of the Holy Spirit. For this reason, we are instructed in the Bible to lay hands upon those who are sick in order that they may be healed (Mark 16:17-18). James wrote that the elders of the church should anoint the sick person with oil and pray a prayer of faith (James 5:14-15). Through such prayer we access and release the very power of God for healing.

We can see how each aspect of this form of prayer is important. The laying on of hands is literally *a point of contact* for spiritual energy to flow from a Christian into the sick person. As the "believing" Christian prays a prayer of faith, the spiritual life flows. Oil applied to the forehead seems to increase the transmission of power, and we can understand this as we watch how people seem to "melt" (that is, become more receptive) as oil is placed upon them. Elders of the church should be mature enough so that they can understand these spiritual principles and actually pray a prayer of faith which releases God's power. Elders have the added authority which not only avails them of God's authority, but tends to make the sick person receive more freely and actually submit to the spiritual flow coming into them through the laying on of hands.

In summary, we re-emphasize that the Christian today should see this whole picture in perspective of health. The physical body does not exist in isolation in the natural world. We treat medically that which can and should be so treated, but health involves the entire being and its association with the spiritual world. The God-given spiritual energy within must be released. To accomplish this the soul may have to be renewed and refocused. The spirit itself can be built up and strengthened. Spiritual energy from others can support and increase vitality. Christians should cleanse themselves of all defilement of flesh and spirit. If any demonic activity is involved, a Christian can exercise authority in the name of Jesus. Finally, God's Holy Spirit can be released through prayer and the laying on of hands. We, as Christians today, do not completely embrace the modern holistic approach, but we do see man as a "whole person," and we must deal with the body, soul, and spirit when speaking of physical healing and health.

Your Spiritual Lifeline

We now can examine how the breath of God within man influences daily decisions, desires, and destiny. Your understanding and application of these principles can alter your future dramatically.

Let's start from the beginning one more time.

When God breathed His spiritual energy into Adam, He released power to give life to all the generations to follow. As we quoted earlier from the Book of Acts, God "...made from one, every nation of mankind to live on all the face of the earth, having determined their appointed times, and the boundaries of their habitation..." (Acts 17:26). The spiritual substance of life exists in our forefathers and is passed on from generation to generation, until the appointed day and place of our beginning.

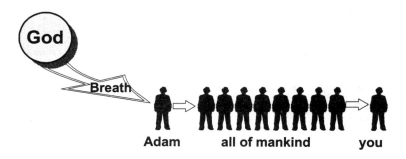

The spiritual substance not only contains information about "appointed times and places" (Acts 17:26), but also about the very purposes of God for our lives. Before God released that breath into Adam, He already had decided the purpose for each individual. The Apostle Paul explained that God has established from the foundations of the world the works that we should fulfill while alive on this earth:

> For we are His workmanship, created in Christ Jesus for good works, which God prepared beforehand, that we should walk in them (Eph. 2:10).

This verse, along with others (i.e., Rom. 9:20-23), tells us that God had us in mind before He created this world, and that He pre-planned what you and I should do while alive on this earth.

This does not mean that we are predestined in the sense of having no free will. Everyone has a free will. What is inherent in the spiritual substance which we receive is the spiritual energy — the grace — the empowerment — necessary to carry out His plan. We each are born with certain gifts, talents, and abilities in line with His desires for our lives. However, we make daily decisions throughout our lifetime whether to walk out the path of grace, use the talents we have, or to "kick against the goads" and resist the will of God.

What is important to see is that no human being is made by accident. God has a plan for creating every single person, and that plan was in the mind of God from the foundations of the world. As God fathered all of mankind, He birthed His will and purposes for each one as He released that original spiritual breath into Adam.

So then, we see that the spiritual breath of God contained not only the power to create each person, but also the *information* relating to the unique plan of God for each life.

This is paralleled in the natural by how genetic material is passed from parent to child. As the genetic code carries with it characteristics from parents to child, so also the spiritual substance, which is passed on from generation to generation, carries with it the information necessary for the design of a person's spiritual characteristics. What happens in the natural is a reflection of what happens in the spiritual.

We use the terminology *spiritual lifeline* to refer to the spiritual substance that has been passed through the generations and becomes available to an individual.

Spiritual Lifeline

Do not think of the spiritual lifeline as fixed or unchanging. What your parents, grandparents and others before you have done may have altered the substance which you receive.

The first example of this is from the life of Adam. When he sinned, the spiritual substance of life became tainted with sin. That which has been passed on has been altered in nature from how God originally released it.

Not only Adam, but all those who have gone ahead of us have, to some degree, changed the spiritual substance we receive. God tells us:

> "...I, the Lord your God, am a jealous God, visiting the iniquity of the fathers on the children, on the third and the fourth generations of those who hate Me, but showing lovingkindness to thousands, to those who love Me and keep My commandments" (Ex. 20:5-6).

Evil can be released upon generations which follow. This is what is meant when the term "generational curses" is used.

Blessings can follow the same way.

We can see several clear examples of this in the Bible. Earlier we mentioned Hebrews 7:9-10, which relates how Abraham brought an offering to Melchizedek; and how Levi, who was still unborn, entered into this blessing. Hannah was a barren woman who vowed to give her child to God if He would open her womb (I Sam. 1:11); this vow of Hannah brought the birth of the prophet Samuel and the calling of God upon his life. Abraham received a blessing which carried with it the favor of God for all the generations to follow him.

It is eye-opening to see how blessings actually can shift from one group of descendants to another. For example, Isaac had two sons, Esau and Jacob. Isaac's blessings were intended for his son Esau, but Esau sold his birthright to his brother Jacob for a meal (Heb. 12:16; Gen. 27). As a consequence, the blessings of God which flowed through the father actually came upon Jacob and his descendants

God's Blessing

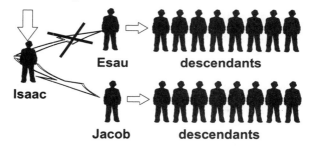

What we can learn from such examples is that the spiritual substance of life can be altered to some degree by those who have gone on ahead of us. Of course, God actually may not be altering the substance passed on in every case. He may sovereignly reach down from heaven during the lifetime of the individual and alter the course of his life, in accordance with the actions of parents. What we do want to recognize, however, is that in some cases the actual spiritual substance that is passed on is changed.

Now, we want to introduce the idea that this principle applies not only in our relationship with God, but in many of the other actions and desires of our forefathers. What your parents did and desired altered what substance you have within you right now. What you do will influence the substance of life passed on to your children.

Consider again the principle of the heart being the fountainhead of a person's life. We all draw in evil through lust, or the opposite, good, through holy desires. That which is drawn into our being spiritually may be passed on to future generations.

Sometime this is true in regard to dreams and desires that are not fulfilled in one's lifetime. For example, a mother may have wished all her life to visit foreign countries, however, due to circumstances, she may never have received the opportunities. What can happen as a result is that her daughter may have the substance of that same desire within her. Therefore, when the daughter grows up she finds a motivation from within, inspiring and pushing her to do what her mother always dreamed of doing.

We can see this spiritual transfer in the life of King David. With all his heart he wanted to build a temple for the worship of God. He was not allowed to do this, but his son, Solomon, received the wisdom, power, authority, and wealth to complete that dream.

This type of passed-on desire can be seen in the lives of many people. It is often the unfulfilled or frustrated dream that appears in the heart of a descendant. For example, a man may live in poverty all of his life, but despises the trap in which he finds himself, constantly desiring to be free; although he never escapes during his lifetime, he may have a son who appears driven to success and financial prosperity. In a similar fashion, evil desires may appear one, two, or three generations later, compelling the recipient to act out that for which his forefather or foremother lusted after.

When we talk about inherited desires, we must not envision them being distributed evenly among one's descendants. Compare this distribution with how physical characteristics are passed on from parent to child. Not every child receives the same features. A mother with red hair may pass on that characteristic to one of her children, while the others may have hair color that resembles their father or grandparents. The genetic code distributes characteristics in a somewhat random manner. In similar fashion we see spiritual characteristics not being distributed uniformly, although we must consider God's involvement in who receives which positive or negative attributes.

It is worth pointing out here that names given to people at birth often are inspired corresponding to inherited characteristics. For example, parents may have a strong desire to name their son after one of his grandfathers; and in many cases, that son will grow up similar in nature to his namesake. This is not stated as an unbreakable rule. We simply are acknowledging a correspondence that sometime can be recognized.

When we talk about the sins of our parents being passed on to us, it is important to note that God said the sins of parents would be visited upon "those who hate Me" (Ex. 20:5). Therefore, the force of evil is not inescapable or inevitable. No. When a person sets his heart against God, that is when the sins of his parents come upon him. The one who loves God will find freedom from the sins of his parents and still receive the positive aspects of their nature.

Furthermore, we need to point out that the negative substance of our parents can be expelled and overcome. When a person, by an act of his will and with the grace of God, rejects some element or characteristic of his parents, he does shield himself from it. Many become free simply by deciding that what their parents did was wrong. Others must make a stronger stand and confess with their mouth that which they cannot accept in their parents. Some find freedom by confessing the sins of their parents to God and accepting personal responsibility for the part they have received.

We are not saying this to put our relationships with parents in a bad light. Please do not think that. The Bible is very clear about honoring our parents. Many characteristics of our parents, especially of godly parents, should be desired, embraced, and received.

Now we can turn our attention to another aspect of our spiritual substance and see that it also can be altered by the people with whom we presently have relationships. We already saw this in the negative sense when Paul exhorted the Corinthian believers to cleanse themselves from all defilement of flesh and spirit (II Cor. 7:1). In the verses preceding this one, Paul warned the Christians not to be bound together with people who were giving themselves to sin or worshipping idols. From this we can learn how the spiritual substance of life within a person can be defiled or made unholy through such relationships.

On the positive side, we are told that when a believer is married to an unbeliever, the presence of the believer to some degree sanctifies that unbeliever (I Cor. 7:14). The spiritual light shines and influences the thoughts and behaviors of the non-Christian. We extend this principle beyond the marriage, because every Christian is a light to the world, and his or her presence should bathe the people around them with the spiritual fragrance of God.

Jesus taught us that people we admire have an especially strong influence upon us. He said,

> "A pupil is not above his teach-
> er; but everyone, after he has
> been fully trained, will be like
> his teacher" (Luke 6:40).

This truth is developed much more fully in Volume IV, but here we simply can say that whenever a person admires and submits to another person, the first will become like the second. This is due in part to a spiritual impartation from the teacher to the student.

We cannot emphasize enough that the heart is the entrance point for spiritual substance. Whenever a person opens their heart to another individual, they are opening it to receive the spiritual influence of that person.

Therefore, a daughter who treasures the photograph of her mother at times will act and think as her mother did, even years after her mother has passed away. A teenage boy who fell in love with a young girl in his school may have a tendency to judge potential mates in the future by the standard of his "first love."   An adult Christian who admired his Sunday School teacher as a child, may cling to the teachings of that Sunday School teacher to such a degree that only the strongest, most persuasive arguments in the future can dislodge those thought patterns. A young girl may bond with a friend and, as a consequence, desire to wear similar clothes, own similar household items, and even fix her hair in similar fashion.

What we see from such examples is that each time a person opens their heart to another, they are offering an entrance point for the influence of that person.   The spiritual impact may alter desires, thoughts, and behavior for years afterward.

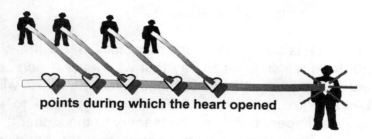

points during which the heart opened

The conclusion we draw from all of this is that the behavior, thoughts, and actions of every human being are very much determined by the influences acting upon their spirit. Some characteristics and forces were built into the nature of a person from the beginning, when God breathed into Adam that first breath of life. Other characteristics are incorporated into the spiritual substance through the thoughts and desires of those who have gone ahead of us. Present relationships also play a major role. Finally, we also must include the will of the individual himself, as he draws in spiritual substances, or yields to the spiritual influences acting upon him. All of these spiritual forces work together to determine the decisions, desires, and destiny of every person.

Still we are not done. In the next chapter, we will discuss how to release and increase the spiritual energy within. We also will see that the spiritual lifeline is not established just in the past, nor only significant for the present, but actually extends into your future. Therefore, you can alter the spiritual substance which will be available to you in the days ahead.

The Breath of God in Us

10
Releasing and Increasing Spiritual Energy

The final question we need to answer now is, "How can we release and increase this spiritual energy within ourselves?"

In addition to the influences discussed in the preceding chapter, we can talk about our ongoing relationship with God. Through the work of the Holy Spirit, God will empower and energize our spirit. Earlier we quoted Ephesians 3:16, where we heard Paul's prayer:

> ...that He would grant you, according to the riches of His glory, to be strengthened with power through His Spirit in the inner man.

God may deposit new anointings, gifts, empowerings, etc., into your spirit. Furthermore, there is an overall energizing effect that can take place within, as we bring our will in line with God's.

The Breath of God in Us

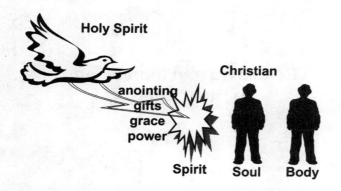

We see many examples of this in the Bible. The Spirit came upon various leaders to give them great wisdom, authority, and leadership abilities. The Spirit of God even came upon Samson to strengthen his physical body (i.e., Judges 14:6,19). When the Spirit came upon David, he was enabled to write the Psalms. When the Spirit came upon certain prophets, they were inspired to speak the very words of God. On Pentecost Day the Holy Spirit came upon the disciples, and they were transformed from weak, timid people into bold witnesses of Jesus Christ. In the Book of Acts we can read about the Spirit filling people such as Paul and giving him authority to rebuke people controlled by devils (i.e., Acts 13:9-10). God's Spirit descended upon people in many ways in Bible times, and they were empowered to accomplish great tasks.

We also are aware of the fact that the devil can give people various spiritual strengths and abilities. In the Book of Acts we can read about two magicians, Simon and Elymus, who demonstrated various supernatural powers (Acts 8:9-11; 13:8-10). A woman at Macedonia was enabled by a demonic spirit to foretell the future (Acts 16:16). The man possessed by a legion of devils was able to break the chains with which he repeatedly was bound (Luke 8:29). From such examples, we can see that devils can, and do, increase the spiritual energies of certain people.

Devil

Spirit   Soul   Body

At the same time, devils also may attack and diminish the strength of individuals. We are told in Ephesians 6:12 that our struggle is not against flesh and blood, but against spiritual beings that can actually harm us. As a Christian encounters evil spiritual authorities, his spirit may recoil and be weakened. When a devil is oppressing a person, his entire being may lose strength.

It is not enough for us simply to categorize all spiritual energies as coming from God or the devil. As we have been explaining, every human is created with a spirit which, indeed, does energize his being. Not only can people have an increase of spiritual energy by the enablement of God or the devil, but they also may release a greater flow from within themselves.

The Breath of God in Us

The spiritual flow is strongest in people who have an *agreement* throughout their entire being. We use the term *agreement* because it accurately describes the condition in which a person's thoughts, emotions, desires, and whole being correspond and work together. Notice we are not talking here about being in agreement with another person, nor even with God. Those are important but they are entirely different subjects. The agreement about which we are speaking here is in reference to all the elements within an individual's body, soul, and spirit. If a person's physical desires correspond with his inner desires, then he will have greater spiritual energy available to him. If a person has beliefs, emotions, and thoughts all directed down the same path, then he will have strong spiritual energies flowing through him. In contrast, a person filled with doubts, under stress, confused, and unsure about what he is doing, will quench the flow from within himself.

For this reason, people who have clear goals in life will have greater spiritual strength, authority, confidence, and effectiveness in this world. People who are bold and outgoing will have stronger flows of spiritual energy. Those who have singleness of focus in their lives, generally speaking, will be healthier, stronger, and more emotionally sound.

We also can talk about specific areas in our lives that need to change in order to increase the spiritual flow. For example, some people have thoughts fixed in their minds that block the flow of life. As people renew their minds to certain truths, they may become set free and, as a result, be able to experience more strength, joy, and peace. Others may have wounds within their character from bad past experiences, and the related scars hinder them from stepping out in faith, going ahead in life, or succeeding in the various endeavors they embrace. Fears and wrong thinking patterns must be overcome for a greater release of the flowing spiritual energy.

Weak Spiritual Flow

Spirit   Soul   Body

These principles are just as true for the non-Christian as they are for the Christian. Of course, the believer has the added dimension of God's Spirit in union with his, but both Christians and non-Christians can release greater measures of the spiritual energy within by bringing their entire being into agreement. The non-Christian who is confident, bold, sure of what he believes (even if it is wrong), focused, active, etc., will have rivers flowing from his innermost being. Anyone who allows the spiritual energy to flow freely will be more alive, successful, able to think, healthy, vibrant, etc.

Many non-Christians are aware of this principle, though they may not understand that spiritual power is involved. Many are trying actively to release the strength and creativity within themselves. There are all kinds of methods, from meditation practices, to relaxing techniques, to positive-thinking exercises. All of them, in some way, attempt to release the energy resident within a person.

Notice we neither are condemning nor condoning any such methods at this time. In Volume V and VI we will discuss such methods more in-depth and explain how and when they may be used rightly or wrongly. Here we simply are trying to show the reality of how spiritual energy from within can be released in greater measure by a person bringing his being into agreement — body, soul and spirit.

From the Biblical perspective, we can identify many other ways by which we can increase the flow of spiritual energy. To name a few, we can list forgiving others, thinking on good things, praying in tongues (I Cor. 14:4), having vision, being active, resting when we need it, helping others, trusting God, etc. In contrast, we could say that sin decreases spiritual strength, for we know that the wages — or the consequences — of sin is death, including depression, discouragement, defeat, etc. Simply living as God wants us to live in our daily lives is the best way to release the spiritual life from within our innermost being.

When we talk about agreement throughout, one of the most significant areas is related to a person's self-identity. For example, an athlete who can boldly declare from the depth of his being, "I am an athlete!"

will have much greater spiritual energy available to him than the one who does not know his role in life. An intelligent young girl who knows she is above average will have greater creative abilities and determination. Similarly, a Christian who knows with full assurance that he is a child of God, will have increased boldness and more energy than the Christian who struggles with his own identity in Christ.

The general attitude a person has about himself is a primary key in determining spiritual strength. When an individual condemns himself, his own spirit diminishes in strength. As one's conscious mind is focused on all the negative aspects of life, the soul shuts down the flow of life and the spirit within is quenched.

Just as the focus of the mind affects the spirit of a man, so also the human body influences the spirit within. We have tried to give a picture of man as a three-part being, yet functioning as a unit. One part cannot be changed without altering the entire man. When people are physically ill, their spirits are typically weakened. On the other hand, when people are healthy and take care of their bodies, it has a positive effect upon their spirits. In First Samuel 30:12, we even can read about a starving man whose "spirit revived" after he ate food. Whatever happens to the outer man influences the inner man.

Fulfilled desires also play a role in the strength of one's spirit (Prov. 13:12). A person who is succeeding at attaining his goals in life is likely to mount up with greater and greater spiritual energy. On the other hand, "...when the heart is sad, the spirit is broken" (Prov. 15:13). Since the heart is the fountainhead from which spiritual energy flows, the health of one's heart establishes the strength of that flow.

Closely related is the will of each person. Some people live in constant indecision, and therefore are spiritually impotent. Decisive people have more spiritual strength available to them on a consistent basis. The Bible tells us that the double-minded person should not expect to receive the blessings of God (James 1:6-7). Some strengths within the spirit of a person will not manifest fully until a firm, authoritative decision is made. Often the individual must speak out boldly or assertively act upon what he believes, before that which is within begins to flow out of him. The power of decision produces an agreement throughout one's being so that spiritual energy begins to flow.

The authority of man's will is surpassed only by one feature within his being: *the imagination*. The truth of this statement is dependent upon the definitions we use for the terms *will* and *imagination*. When we speak of man's will in this context, we are referring to the ability to make present decisions. We are using this term in *the narrow sense of choices that can be made to do good or bad right at the moment of decision*. This aspect of man's will, we will see, is not as powerful as man's imagination.

When we speak of the *imagination,* we are speaking of the pictures, impressions, and images moving within the spirit of a person. We also are talking about man's ability to form and meditate on those pictures.

The word *imagination* is used with different meanings in other contexts. Christians sometime have negative connotations that are associated with this term, because they are using it in reference to vain imaginations. These are carnal and we are warned against them in the Bible (II Cor. 10:5). Here we are referring specifically to the spiritual impressions which arise from within a person. Some of these are good and some of these are bad; but now we will see how all of them are powerful.

Consider George, a man who has been under financial stress all of his life. Deep in his heart, he believes that he always will be poor and broke. He was raised with a view of himself as poor, and he cannot break that vision within his own mind. No matter what he tries to do by an act of his will, nothing works out successfully for him in the area of finances. We see in actual experience that his will is not as powerful as his vision.

Next think of Bill, a man who has been entertaining lustful thoughts in his mind and heart for several months. As the Bible teaches us, his lusts will conceive that evil within him. One day when the circumstances make sexual sin available to him, Bill will be unable to resist. His will shall not be powerful enough to keep him from engaging in the sexual act. We see then that Bill's will is not as strong as his imagination.

Finally, consider Mike. He has been meditating day after day about building a home for his family. Several years have gone by and he has built that home in his visions time and time again. One day when the opportunity arises, he is going to find tremendous spiritual energy rising within his heart actually to carry out that task. Through his years of meditating on this project, he has been increasing the spiritual energy which shall be available to him in the future.

What a person envisions today, he will enact tomorrow. Proverbs 23:7a tells us:

> For as he thinks within himself,
> so he is.

The imaginations of your heart are forming your future.

The power of this truth is made clear when we grasp the whole concept of man, which we have developed throughout this volume. The spiritual substance resident in every human being is divine in origin. It not only gives us life, but contains within it *creative power*. Wherever a person's heart is directed is where his spiritual energy goes. It is forming the world around him and establishing his future.

Allow me to impact you with this final truth.

Recall how God first created the world. Before He spoke anything into existence, we are told that His Spirit brooded (moved or hovered) over the surface of the waters (Gen. 1:2). The word *brooded* is the same word which describes a mother hen patiently nesting and warming her eggs. Here, of course, we are talking about something much more holy, powerful, and divine. The Spirit of God was moving across the earth preparing it for the creative acts about to take place.

The amazing truth is that the same spiritual, creative substance which first moved over the earth was deposited in Adam — and then passed on to all mankind. Some of that *God stuff* is in each one of us.

Furthermore, we were created in God's image. When we say this we are not putting ourselves on an equal level with God — of course not! We can understand this relationship better by seeing how a model airplane may be designed after the image of a real airplane. In similar fashion, God has designed us after His image.

As God has creative power within Him, so also do we. As the Spirit of God emanates out of Him, so also the spirit within man emanates out. The spiritual energy within man is not a stagnant, fixed substance. As it is released from within, it flows like a river of energy, influencing the world around us.

Spirit/Soul/Body

When a person envisions things, he is releasing spiritual energy to accomplish the related goals. The greater his faith, agreement within, and determination, the greater will be the flow of spiritual energy acting upon the natural world.

We will learn how this functions in Volumes IV to VI. Here our primary point is that the spiritual energy, indeed can be released in greater measure by the visions we have within us. Visions can be changed and, hence, the release of spiritual energy can be altered.

The "How to's" of all this, along with countless other spiritual concepts, we are saving for the volumes which follow this one. We purposely are writing this information volume by volume in order to hold and stimulate your interest. I hope to plant within you visions of what the future volumes hold, knowing that your vision will be more powerful than your will.

Conclusion

The single most profound truth we have discovered in this volume is that God's breath resides in us. We each have a deposit of this divinely originated substance, and it provides every human being with the energy necessary to live. We also learned how the release of that energy within man influences his emotional well-being, ability to think, physical health, daily decisions, and overall effectiveness in life.

We also have introduced the concepts that spiritual energy is creative and that it can flow from out of man to influence the world around him. These foundational truths give us keys to understanding many spiritual experiences, demonstrations of supernatural power, paranormal experiences, and other phenomena which we will explain in coming volumes.

What is your question?

Although several volumes of this series already have been released, there are later volumes at various stages of completion. If you have questions related to the spiritual realm which you wish to have answered, feel free to submit your questions to our office, and we will consider addressing them in future volumes. We would love to hear from you.

Winepress Publishing
P.O. Box 10653
Yakima, WA, 98909-1653, USA

Or E-mail to: winepress@nwinfo.net

Books by Harold R. Eberle, available from Winepress Publishing, include the following:

Spiritual Realities
Volume I: The Spiritual World and How We Access It
Volume II: The Breath of God in Us
Volume III: Escaping Dualism
(Volumes IV-VII are in various stages of completion)

Developing a Prosperous Soul
Volume I: How to Overcome a Poverty Mind-set
Volume II: How to Walk in God's Financial Blessings

The Complete Wineskin* (Restructuring the Church for the Outpouring of the Holy Spirit)
The Living Sword (Applying the Word of God to Current Controversial Issues, such as Women in Ministry, Divorce and Remarriage, etc.)
Two Become One* (Releasing God's Power for Romance, Sexual Freedom and Blessings in Marriage)
God's Leaders For Tomorrow's World (Understanding Leadership Dynamics, Dealing with Power Struggles and Developing Personal Leadership Abilities)

*Also available as an audiobook on cassette tape.

For current prices or to place an order by phone, call:
1-800-308-5837 within the USA or **509-308-5837** from outside the USA (MasterCard/VISA accepted).

Winepress Publishing
P.O. Box 10653, Yakima, WA 98989-10653, USA

E-mail: winepress@nwinfo.net
http://www.grmi.org/ministry/winepress/